FIELDS OF POISON

Migrant Farmworker to Crusading Physician

D1602334

Michael Halperin

Floricanto Press

Floricanto is a trademark of *Floricanto Press.*

Berkeley Press is an imprint of Inter-American Development, Inc.

Floricanto Press

7177 Walnut Canyon Rd.

Moorpark, California 93021

(415) 793-2662

www.FloricantoPress.com

ISBN: 978-0-915745-21-0

Library of Congress Control Number: 2020934314

"Por nuestra cultura hablarán nuestros libros. Our books shall speak for our culture."

Roberto Cabello-Argandoña and Leyla Namazie, Editors

Reviews: *Fields of Poison*

"Fields of Poison relates the dramatic account of battles encountered by Dr. Antonio Velasco in seeking social and legal justice to protect workers from highly hazardous pesticides. The early chapters provide a vivid account of his life and struggles as a Mexican immigrant seeking education and work in the United States. Despite constraints, he became a medical doctor who focused on the mismanagement of pesticides that exposed farm workers to highly toxic insecticides. The first pesticide named is aldrin (page 100) as crop residues far exceeded the maximum permitted. Rachel Carson's article in the New York Times about the misuse of pesticides subsequently published as a book Silent Spring (1962) led to banning organochlorine insecticides and other Persistent Organic Pesticides. Unfortunately, the ban resulted in using more organophosphorus insecticides! When César Chávez of the United Farm Workers informed Dr. Velasco that 'Pesticides pose the greatest risk to farm workers', he took action after diagnosing farm workers poisoned by a mixture of phosdrin (normally called mevinphos) and Phosphamidon. The World Health Organisation classified both pesticides as Class Ia extremely toxic insecticides. Dr. Velasco and his team of scientists succeeded in passing legislation to protect farm workers. However, in American courts lawyers and non-scientists tend to protect industry rather than support sustainable and safe use of less hazardous pesticides. Farmers in the European Union are urged to adopt integrated pest management. Pesticides are a last resort."

Graham Matthews, Ph.D., DSc. Emeritus Professor of Pest Management, Imperial College, London, UK. Advisor to the World Health Organization; Technical Director NGO Yaounde Initiative Foundation, Cameroon. Author: History of Pesticides; Pesticides: Health Safety and the Environment; Integrated Vector Management; Pesticide Application Methods 3rd Edition; Pest management.

"Fields of Poison is a moving and important portrayal of the life and impact of Dr. Antonio Velasco, a migrant farmworker who became a physician and dedicated his life to serving those in need. The book is a detailed and significant portrait of human courage and the potential that lies within us all to learn from personal suffering and to substantively contribute to the larger good. Fields of Poison takes the reader through Dr. Velasco's life in an intimate, yet measured manner, detailing his struggles and following his career as he makes groundbreaking discoveries regarding how to identify and treat pesticide exposure and how to live a morally grounded life. It is a significant book about an unsung American hero and an especially important contribution in these difficult times."

Daniel Rothenberg, Ph.D. Professor of Practice, School of Politics and Global Studies; Co-Director, Center on the Future of War, Arizona State University, Tempe; Senior Fellow, New America. Author: With These Hands: The Hidden World of Migrant Farmworkers Today.

"With detailed research and reporting Fields of Poison tells the story of the extraordinary brilliance and tenacity of Dr. Antonio Velasco in overcoming systemic racism and injustice in America. His story reminds us it is possible to bend the arc of history towards justice. From his earliest days as a child immigrant laboring in California's fields to fighting for the right to study medicine Dr. Velasco's courage and perseverance provides the inspiration to never give up battling for yourself and others. He formed a team to diagnose the cause of the near-death state of poisoned workers dumped outside his hospital and provided them lifesaving treatment. What raises this beyond a remarkable personal struggle is that Dr. Velasco went further to protect farm workers and their families from pesticide poisoning. Endangering his career and family he called out Big Ag and the pesticide industry to ensure that truth was told. He fought for and helped pass regulations and laws that required posting warnings of fields recently sprayed with dangerous chemicals. Dr. Velasco designed new laboratory methods to identify and assess levels of pesticides in the blood and protocols for treatment and taught these methods to doctors, clinics and hospitals across the country. Dr. Velasco's life is the story of our public heroes overcoming personal obstacles and serving others."

Harry Snyder, J.D. Advocacy Leader in Residence, University of California School of Public Health.

ACKNOWLEDGMENTS

My thanks to Antonio Velasco for entrusting me with his heroic story. I wish to also thank those who contributed their recollections and assisted with research.

Meyo Velasco-López
Clayton Abajian
Jeff Solinas, M.D.
Isabel Guzmán Velasco
James Coleman, M.D.
California Sen. William Monning
Antonio Ruelas, M.D.
Frank Meza, M.D.
José Alberto Arévalo, M.D.
Charlie Clements, M.D., MPH
Luisa Buada
Juan Martínez
Ira Monossan, M.D.
Delia Saldívar, Radio Bilingüe
Kathleen Esdaile
Elva García Rendón
Tranquilino Rendón, Jr.
Monterey Herald
Natividad Medical Center
Salinas *Californian*
California Rural Legal Assistance

Southern California Library for Social Studies and Research

Charles E. Young Research Library, University of California Los Angeles

California Department of Food and Agriculture

California Department of Pest Regulation

California Department of Industrial Relations

John Steinbeck Library, Salinas, California

Special thanks to my editor, proofreader, and wife, Marcia Halperin without whom this book would not exist.

CONTENTS

PREFACE

The University of California, Santa Cruz transformed a rock quarry into an amphitheater surrounded by a verdant redwood forest blanketed with giant ferns where a diverse body of students received their diplomas. The university president proudly introduced the keynote speaker Santa Cruz's Humanitarian of the Year, Antonio R. Velasco, M.D.

A diminutive, slight man with a sly smile walked to the lectern and carefully moved the microphone down so he could be heard. In a voice inflected with a dialect reflecting his upbringing in the western highlands of Mexico he recounted a remarkable odyssey to America with his migrant farmworker family. Determined not to become dependent on the rise and fall of harvest seasons he used his intellect and curiosity to overcome enormous odds and became a physician and scientist. Dr. Velasco's story resonated with the struggle almost every immigrant experiences

When the cultural climate toward immigrants in America changed I contacted Dr. Velasco and proposed writing his story with two purposes in mind. One was a scientific detective story investigating a multitude of pesticide poisoning incidents among migrant farmworkers. The other story emphasizes that America's strength comes from its diverse population. His story is one of courage and perseverance against enormous odds. Dr. Velasco feels compelled that as someone who rose out of farm fields and achieved success in the healing profession he must defend the thousands of workers who toil in fields, orchards, on farms and in factories to provide our nation with food and goods but who yield little political power.

    Michael Halperin

Chapter One

Consequences

Tumultuous events reverberated in the complex, conflicted relations between Mexico and the United States for two-and-a-half centuries. Border struggles impacted with ferocity the lives of Mexican nationals and Mexican Americans into the 21st Century. Evolving and often contentious relations mirrored the rise of the American republic.

The British Empire dominated the continent in the 18th century from the northern region of New France (Canada) to Spanish Florida. Spain reigned over Central America, Mexico, and half of America from the Pacific to the Mississippi River enfolding what we know as Texas, New Mexico, Arizona, Colorado, Wyoming and most of California. The French controlled not only Canada but also territory to the south with its prize New Orleans, the major southern port on the Gulf of Mexico.

Thirteen British colonies huddling along the east coast of America rebelled against the injustice of monarchical rule with a searing Declaration of Independence in 1776. After eight grueling years the British Empire, exhausted by the cost of war three-thousand miles from its homeland, surrendered. American colonists defeated Great Britain and won their independence.

Wars, intrigue, and political chicanery influenced political decisions and determined interactions between Mexico and the United States for generations. The American Revolution sparked rebellion in France leading to the blood-soaked destruction of the monarchy that eventually brought Napoleon Bonaparte to power.

Spurred by the Spanish occupation of Mexico in the nineteenth century Catholic cleric Miguel Hidalgo y Costilla led a failed rebellion. Father Miguel's execution at the hands of Spain invigorated revolutionary ire. Mexico gained independence in 1822 and crowned as emperor the leader of its army General Agustín de Iturbide. After a short reign democratic factions forced Iturbide off the throne. Attempts at democracy continued to persist through years of turmoil.

Bribery, mismanagement and corruption beset Mexican independence founded on the American experiment. While in the United States political parties vied for votes within a constitutional democratic framework, Mexico bore the weight of Spanish and French traditions that resisted centralized leadership. It also had an indigenous, suspicious, anti-assimilationist population that opposed the Mexican power structure.

Then as now major obstacles existed along the border. Mexico made far-reaching decisions to settle many of its citizens in the north. The country also engaged in a pro-immigrant program promising land along with civil and property rights to white Europeans who converted to Catholicism. Having abolished slavery thirty-nine years before the Emancipation Proclamation announced by President Abraham Lincoln in 1863, Mexico made the same offer of land and rights to slaves escaping bondage in America. With the lure of large tracts of ranch land Europeans, former slaves and white settlers clustered on the border. To the Mexican government's chagrin they rarely integrated into society. Mexico could not muster the political will to force them to adopt their culture, history or tradition.

Native Americans refused to recognize national borders since tribal territories overlapped the border between the United States and Mexico. For the sake of maintaining a tentative peace they signed multiple treaties with the federal government in Washington.

Chief Speckled Snake of the Creek nation predicted an ominous future for his people during the administration of Andrew Jackson.

"Brother! I have listened to a great many talks from our Great Father [the President]. But they always begin and end in this—'Get a little farther; you are too near to me.'"[1]

"In the early 1830s, following what for most had been nearly two generations of imperfect peace, Comanche, Kiowa, Navajo, and several different tribes of Apaches dramatically increased attacks upon northern Mexican settlements. While contexts and motivations varied widely, most of the escalating violence reflected Mexico's declining military and diplomatic capabilities, as well as burgeoning markets for stolen livestock and captives. Indian men raided Mexican ranches, haciendas, and towns, killing or capturing the people they found there, and stealing or destroying animals and other property. When able, Mexicans responded by attacking their enemies with comparable cruelty and avarice. Raids expanded breeding reprisals and deepening enmities.

"These events had powerful but virtually forgotten consequences for the course and outcome of the U.S.-Mexican

War. In pursuing their own material, strategic, and cultural goals, indigenous polities in the Mexican north remade the ground upon which Mexico and the United States would compete in the mid-1840s. Raids and counter-raids claimed thousands of lives, ruined critical sectors of northern Mexico's economy, stalled the North's demographic growth, depopulated much of its vast countryside, and fueled divisive conflicts between Mexicans at nearly every level of political integration." [2]

Former President Andrew Jackson, under whose administration in 1829 ordered the forced expulsion of Native Americans from their homeland in the south to west of Mississippi, upheld the pretext that Britain and the Republic of Mexico plotted a political alliance against the United States. Jackson came out of retirement and announced his support for the annexation of Texas: "…peaceably if we can, forcibly if we must."[3]

Kentucky Senator Henry Clay ran for president in 1843 against the expansionist candidate of the Democratic Party, James Polk. The esteemed sixth President of the United States John Quincy Adams determined to continue serving his country was elected to the House of Representatives from Massachusetts. Agitated that the United States would consider annexing a major portion of Mexico, Adams with Ohio Representative Joshua Giddings and other members of the House Foreign Affairs Committee issued the scathing, "An Address to the People of the Free States" denouncing an invasion of a sovereign nation, Mexico, by the United States with the intent of annexing the Mexican state of Texas and using the pretext of war as an excuse to expand the reach of slavery.

It stated: "We hold there is no political necessity for it, no advantage to be derived from it, but think there is no constitutional power delegated to any department of the National Government to authorize it. That no act of Congress or treaty for annexation can impose the least obligation upon several States of the Union to submit to such an unwarrantable act, or to receive into their family and fraternity such misbegotten and illegitimate progeny. We hesitate not to say, that annexation, effected by any act or proceeding of the Federal Government, or any of its departments, will be identified with dissolution. We not only assert the people of the free States ought not to submit to it, but we say with confidence they will not submit to it."[4]

Polk, an avid exponent for the annexation of Texas that proclaimed itself an independent republic unacknowledged by Mexico, won the 1844 election. Eager to bring Texas into the pro-slavery orbit, he unilaterally signed the Texas Admission Act, Dec. 29, 1845. The preface of the act stated: "Resolved by the Senate and House of Representatives of the United States of America in Congress assembled, That Congress doth consent that the territory properly included within and rightfully belonging to the Republic of Texas, may be erected into a new State to be called the State of Texas..."[5]

Subsequently Polk declared war on Mexico in an address to Congress:

"The existing state of the relations between the United States and Mexico renders it proper that I should bring the subject to the consideration of ... Congress...The Mexican government invaded our territory and shed the blood of our fellow citizens on our own soil... The invasion was threatened solely because Texas had determined... to annex herself to our Union and under these circumstances it was plainly our duty to extend our protection over her citizens and soil.

"Accordingly on the 13th of January (1846) last instructions were issued to the general in command of these troops to occupy the left bank of the Del Norte [Rio Grande]. Anticipating the possibility of... threatened invasion, authorizing General Taylor... to accept volunteers, not from Texas only, but from the States of Louisiana, Alabama, Mississippi, Tennessee, and Kentucky... General Taylor was further 'authorized by the President to make requisition upon the executive of that state for such of its militia force as may be needed to repel invasion or to secure the country against apprehended invasion'...I invoke the prompt action of Congress to recognize the existence of war."[6]

In 1846. Zachary Taylor moved into Texas, ignoring Mexico's insistence American troops marching to the Rio Grande pull back. Alarmed by the intrusion of an invading army and settlers into what it deemed its sovereign territory, the Mexican government immediately prepared for war.

Clay made a plea against what he considered an ill-conceived armed conflict. "Shall this War be prosecuted for the purpose of conquering and annexing Mexico, in all its boundless extent, to the United States? ... I will not attribute to the President of the United States any other design; but I confess I have been shocked and alarmed by the manifestations of it in

8

various quarters. Of all the dangers and misfortunes that could befall this nation, I should regard that of becoming a warlike and conquering power the most direful and fatal...That the power of the United States is competent to the conquest of Mexico is quite possible. But it could not be achieved without frightful carnage, dreadful sacrifice of human life..."[7]

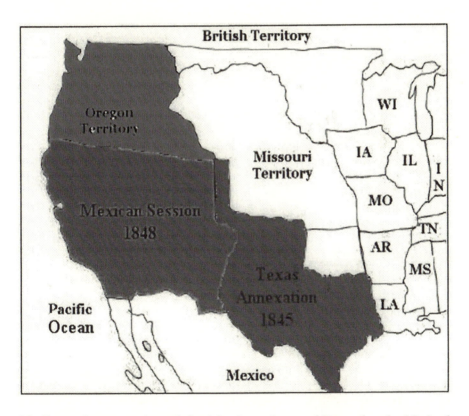

Unilateral annexation of the Mexican State of Texas by the United States, 1845. Mexican Session via Treaty of Guadalupe Hidalgo, 1848.

The war culminated in the signing of the 1848 Treaty of Guadalupe Hidalgo between the United States and Mexico. Mexico lost fifty-five percent of its territory. Texas, Arizona,

California, New Mexico, Utah along with large swaths of Colorado and Wyoming became American territories.

The Gadsden Purchase, 1854. United States purchased 29,670 square miles solidifying the current border with Mexico (Contemporary map used for reference)

The United States purchased in 1854 an additional 29,670 square miles in the region of present-day Arizona and New Mexico that established the current border. Known as the Gadsden Purchase, it was brokered and signed by the U.S. ambassador to Mexico James Gadsden and the president of Mexico Antonio López de Santa Anna. [8]

One hundred thousand Spanish-speaking Mexicans endured an identity crisis as a result of the Mexican American

War and the Gadsden Purchase. They could retain Mexican citizenship and live as aliens in the United States or gain citizenship at an unspecified date. The preponderance of Mexicans decided to remain in the U.S. resulting in racial discrimination and hardship.

Searching for a savior after years of oppression by an amoral leadership, Mexico elected the brilliant peasant lawyer Benito Juárez president in 1861. By sheer strength of will and incredible confidence he overcame prejudice against what he called *indios de la raza primitiva del país*, Indians of the original race of the country. He became a lawyer, was elected to the city council of Oaxaca and married into a wealthy family with roots in Europe.

Wealthy landed conservatives resented his election, and many fled the country. They pleaded for France to assist their overthrow of Juárez. Napoleon III had expansionist plans for America. He used the dislike and distrust of the president of Mexico to achieve his goals at a time when the United States was riven by the Civil War.

Napoleon III provided Mexican dissidents with troops, finances, and Archduke Maximilian von Habsburg, the brother of the Austrian emperor, who was offered the title Emperor of Mexico. In 1862 the French invaded Mexico and drove Juárez into exile. They placed the ill-equipped, naive Maximilian on the Mexican throne the following year.

At the conclusion of the Union victory over the Confederacy, the United States armed and supported Juárez in his quest to bring democracy back to Mexico. Maximilian was ousted in 1867. Juárez returned to Mexico City and sentenced the archduke to death by firing squad.

After Juárez, administrations in Mexico once again experienced seesaw relations with the United States. Rampant distrust continued until the election of Franklin Delano Roosevelt as President of the United States in 1933.

In his first inaugural address Roosevelt announced a radical change in Western Hemisphere politics. "In the field of world policy I would dedicate this Nation to the policy of the good neighbor—the neighbor who resolutely respects himself and, because he does so, respects the rights of others—the neighbor who respects his obligations and respects the sanctity of his agreements in and with a world of neighbors.

"If I read the temper of our people correctly, we now realize as we have never realized before our interdependence on each other; that we cannot merely take but we must give as well; that if we are to go forward, we must move as a trained and loyal army willing to sacrifice for the good of a common discipline, because without such discipline no progress is made, no leadership becomes effective. We are, I know, ready and willing to submit our lives and property to such discipline, because it makes possible a leadership which aims at a larger good. This I propose to offer, pledging that the larger purposes will bind upon us all as a sacred obligation with a unity of duty hitherto evoked only in time of armed strife."9

The speech became the foundation forming the Good Neighbor Policy originally introduced by President Herbert Hoover and executed by Roosevelt. Mexico tested the policy when it nationalized its foreign controlled oil industry. Determined not to undermine amity with its neighbor, the Roosevelt administration restrained from retaliatory action.

Three years later Roosevelt completed the transformation of the Monroe Doctrine from a unilateral policy to one that embraced all Western Hemisphere nations in a speech at Chautauqua, New York.

"In the whole of the Western Hemisphere our good neighbor policy has produced results that are especially heartening...The American republics to the south of us have been ready always to cooperate with the United States on a basis of equality and mutual respect, but before we inaugurated the good neighbor policy there was among them resentment and fear, because certain administrations in Washington had slighted their national pride and their sovereign rights.

"In pursuance of the good neighbor policy, and because in my younger days I had learned many lessons in the hard school of experience, I stated that the United States was opposed definitely to armed intervention...We have undertaken a series of trade agreements with other American countries to our mutual commercial profit. At the request of two neighboring republics, I hope to give assistance in the final settlement of the last boundary dispute between any of the American nations.... Of all the nations of the world today we are in many ways most singularly blessed. Our closest neighbors are good neighbors. If there are remoter nations that wish us not good but ill, they know we are strong; they know we can and will defend ourselves and defend our neighborhood. We seek to dominate no other nation. We ask no territorial expansion. We oppose imperialism. We desire reduction in world armaments. We believe in democracy; we believe in freedom; we believe in peace. We offer to every nation of the world the handclasp of the good neighbor. Let those who wish our friendship look us in the eye and take our hand." [10]

Prior to World War Two the Axis powers attempted to bring Mexico into their orbit. With the outbreak of World War Two, the U.S. countered with the need to maintain unity against Fascist aggression. Mexico and Brazil joined the United States, Great Britain, and France in May 1942 against the Nazi menace. A quarter million Mexicans and a million Mexican Americans served in the armed forces of the United States.

Thousands of men in cities, towns and on farms of America were drafted into the armed services. Young and older men and women abandoned farms for higher wages in the booming American defense industry.

The flight of farm workers left an immense void that had to be filled for the war effort to succeed. Mexico provided laborers to the United States. They not only contributed to the Allied victory they benefited Mexico economically as workers sent remittances to families south of the border.

In July 1942 Ernesto Hidalgo, representative of Mexico's Foreign Affairs Ministry and Abraham J. Navas, Esq., representative of Mexico's Ministry of Labor met with Joseph F. McGurk, Counsel of the American Embassy in México, John Walker, Deputy Administrator of the Farm Security Administration, United States Department of Agriculture (USDA), and David Mecker, Deputy Director of War Farming Operations also from the USDA.

They signed an Executive Order creating the Mexican Farm Labor Program, [11] commonly called the Bracero Program, between Mexico and the United States. It was the first treaty legalizing and controlling Mexican migrant workers

The program initially was planned to end upon termination of hostilities. At the behest of ranchers, farmers and major agribusiness the United States and

Mexico extended the treaty several times. The unintended consequence of the program not only permitted legal workers entry into the United States it also encouraged thousands of undocumented laborers to enter the country. Paradoxically, many undocumented workers were rounded up by the Texas Employment Commission that delivered them to grower groups throughout Texas and other states in violation of immigration laws and the agreement with Mexico. [12]

In 1951 the Executive Order that created the Bracero program became Public Law 78 amending the last extension of the Agricultural Act of 1949. "Title V-Agricultural Workers" was passed by the House of Representatives and the Senate and signed into law by President Harry Truman.

The preamble to Public Law 78 stated that its purpose was: "For the purpose of assisting in such production of agricultural commodities and products as the Secretary of Agriculture deems necessary, by supplying agricultural workers from the Republic of Mexico (pursuant to arrangements between the United States and Mexico)..."[13]

The treaty and subsequent law did not please everyone. Some viewed imported workers as akin to indentured servants. Pauline R. Kibbe, Executive Secretary of the Good Neighbor Commission of Texas wrote:

"Generally speaking, the Latin-American migratory worker going into west Texas is regarded as a necessary evil, nothing more nor less than an unavoidable adjunct to the harvest season. Judging by the treatment that has been accorded him in that section of the state, one might assume that he is not a human being at all, but a species of farm implement that comes mysteriously and spontaneously into being coincident with the maturing of cotton, that requires no upkeep or special consideration during the period of its usefulness, needs no protection from the elements, and when the crop has been harvested, vanishes into the limbo of forgotten things-until the next harvest season rolls around. He has no past, no future, only a brief and anonymous present."[14]

Under the imprimatur of the Bracero program José Dolores Velasco from a village in the western highlands of Mexico crossed the border into the United States. He joined four hundred forty-five thousand men and women seeking to lift their incomes.

Chapter Two

Under the Volcano

Volcán de Fuego, Colima, Mexico (M. Halperin)

The ever-erupting Volcán de Fuego above the small village of Cofradía de Suchitlán[15] in the highlands of Colima, Mexico paralleled the volatile relationship between José Dolores Velasco, his children, and his wife Teresa. Along with hundreds of thousands of Mexican men, he opted to journey north across the border to work on American farms and orchards in order to lift his earning power.

The money he sent home made life easier for his family, but he took a different road than other migrant farm workers. He remained in the States, *El Norte*, for extended periods of times – years – while other workers journeyed home once or twice a year to spend time with their families. Those absences created a vast chasm in the life of Antonio Velasco, his older brother David and young sister Meyo. Confusion about their father who appeared and disappeared like a ghost or figment of imagination underscored broken ties of affection.

"We didn't know our dad," recalled Antonio. "He had been gone for years to work in the United States and only returned to Mexico a couple of times. He was like a mythical character that became real. It was hard for me as a seven-year old to relate to him."

José Velasco signed up for the Bracero Program after the birth of Antonio in 1953. He left his wife, Teresa, with Antonio and David and traveled to Yuma, Arizona to work in lemon orchards. Along with legal braceros, a host of undocumented workers crossed the border. One year later the United States under the administration of President Dwight Eisenhower reacted against illegal immigration by mounting the derisively titled "Operation Wetback."

A military-style roundup searched and captured illegal immigrants from Mexico. The wholesale sweep of temporary laborers often made no distinction between those without legal documentation and those who entered the country with proper paperwork.

"Beginning from the Rio Grande Valley, 'Wetback' spread quickly; Illegal immigrants were sent back by force and armed military. On July 15, the first day of the 'Wetback',

4,800 illegal immigrants were 'gone'. From the day after, about 1,100 illegal immigrants were sent back per day." [16]

The Los Angeles Committee for the Protection of Foreign Born (LACPFB) formed in 1950 had the goal of preserving the rights of the foreign born. Its founder, Russian born Rose Chernin living in Los Angeles was charged with membership in the Young Communist League and threatened with deportation. Eventually the Supreme Court of the United States reversed her conviction. In the 1950s the committee concentrated on "the plight of legal and illegal Mexicans in Los Angeles, many of whom were deported without due process." [17]

Responding to why she took up the mantle to defend Mexican workers Chernin said: "This struggle of people against their condition, this is where you find the meaning of life."

Josefina Yáñez Executive Secretary of LACPFB commented on 'Operation Wetback': "The role of the immigration authorities—their dragnet operations wherein they swoop down upon fields, factories, and entire communities—is so well-known and feared in any Mexican American that the word 'Los Federales' strikes terror not alone to the non-citizen but to Mexican American citizens of the first, second, and third generations." [18]

Yuma, Arizona lemon ranchers on the vast Sonoran Desert relied on heavy irrigation. During the hot summer months José Velasco harvested lemons. Sharp thorns ripped and tore into hands. Thick leather gloves gave workers a modicum of protection, but thorns pierced gloves and harvesters often ended in hospitals with severe infections.

José's skill devising irrigation plans and repair of canals, ditches and pipelines earned him a Green Card [19] permitting year-round work. Laboring in the United States where wages were higher than anything he could earn in Mexico was a major upward step for the poor farmer from a small village in Colima.

José Velasco "Green Card." Issued 1962 at Nogales, Arizona Port of Entry October 1962. (Velasco Family Archive)

Gregarious and eager to be surrounded by friends and co-workers, José engaged in weekend parties with compadres who indulged in bouts of drinking as a way of deadening the torment of spending twelve to fourteen hours a day under a torrid sun with bodies enduring agonizing pain week after week. Stoic and self-contained when sober, he became amiable and voluble under the influence of liquor.

Cofradía de Suchitlán. Original Velasco home built by Jose Velasco, 1953 (Velasco Family Archive)

He arrived for a brief visit to his hometown of Cofradía de Suchitlán in 1955 flaunting his success in *El Norte* by lavishing his immediate and extended family with gifts and doling out money for daylong drinking parties. After two weeks he returned to Yuma. The same year Antonio's sister Remedio (Meyo) was born.

Four years later he returned briefly to Cofradía. Shortly after José departed for Arizona in 1959 Teresa found she was pregnant once more. She continued working as a health care provider in the area. Six-year old Antonio joined his mother on hikes into the mountains gathering herbs for salves, emetics, and natural cures for colds and headaches.

In late September Teresa visited a physician in Colima, the state capitol. She complained of occasional pain and a few incidents of bleeding. After an examination the doctor recommended terminating the pregnancy out of concern for her health.

Teresa's training from the Mexican Health Department on current medical practices and her assistance in multiple births in Cofradía and neighboring villages provided her an education in medical care that foreshadowed Antonio's future. In her opinion the doctor's diagnosis after a cursory medical screening seemed rash.

Without hesitation she wrote to her mother Rosario who lived in Mexico City with her husband Cirilo Rubio a retired army veteran. Teresa informed Rosario she and the children were coming to the capital city to be seen by a specialist. David, Antonio, and Meyo packed into a bus for the four-hundred-mile journey. It seemed to the children an interminable, dangerous drive to a foreign land.

Forests gave way to green valleys and mountains stretching across the horizon. Temperature precipitously dropped as they steadily climbed higher. Mexico City, situated approximately three miles above sea level, was cold in comparison to their home in the western highlands.

"My memory of the city still seems like a post-apocalyptic black and white movie; dirty, smoggy, smelly, crowded, devoid of any trees or plants, noisy, and dangerous," Antonio reported. "My grandmother Rosario and my mother's step-father Cirilo Rubio lived in a *vecindad*, a walled neighborhood with a big double door entrance, locked and guarded at night, open during the day. It was three stories high, about eighteen units total, with two communal bathrooms on the second floor. The street in front of the complex was unpaved.

"Hills of trash were everywhere. People sifted through putrid garbage collecting huge mounds of cardboard to sell for recycling. With backs bent under the weight they resembled ants scrambling through the debris."

The small first-floor apartment consisted of a twelve-by-twelve bedroom with barred windows. Antonio's grandmother and Cirilo used the double bed. The children slept under the bed. At night their mother lay near them on the floor.

With well-organized gangs roaming the city Cirilo insisted the children not go out in the evening. They believed they were safe behind the locked gates of the *vecindad* until faced by the unexpected.

"Two gang members escaping from the police broke into our unit one night. They ordered us to keep quiet while the guards who were supposed to protect us told the police the robbers had run down the street. The guards gave my grandmother money as a reward and told her they would shield us against gangs from other neighborhoods," Antonio clearly recalled.

As a veteran, Cirilo had the privilege of using military hospitals for members of his family. He arranged for an obstetrician to see Teresa at the Women's Clinic of the Military Hospital in Mexico City. They admitted her for an examination and observation.

Meyo remained with her grandmother during the day. David and Antonio ventured to nearby Chapultepec Park, one of the largest parks in Central and South America. The massive *Castillo de Chapultepec* rose on high knoll. Constructed on the archeologic site of an ancient Aztec building called Casa Denegrida, Black House. Emperor Maximillian I used the castle as his headquarters during his short, tragic reign. In 1939 the government converted it into the National Museum of History, currently the National Museum of Cultures.

Below the castle Antonio and David walked through stately columns surmounted by stylized eagles of the majestic Monument to the *Niños Héroes* a memorial to six teenage Mexican army cadets who died defending the castle against American forces during the Battle of Chapultepec in 1847.

On other days Antonio and David climbed to the roof of their grandmother's complex where they watched traffic crossing a bridge. Green taxicabs with teeth painted on their sides fascinated them.

"We played games to see who could spot one first and yell *cocodrilo* (crocodile)," Antonio recalled fondly. "We had to cross the bridge over a rail line to get to the market. I was terrified to walk over. When my grandmother wanted to take us, I screamed I didn't want to go. David dragged me kicking all the way. There was a reward once we arrived at the market. My grandmother bought us huge cups of chocolate accompanied by wonderful sweet bread."

Teresa gave birth without complications to a daughter also named Teresa on October 19, 1959. They stayed with Rosario and Cirilo for two months before returning to Cofradía de Suchitlán. In the interim Teresa shopped for the children.

"My mother bought David and me leather jackets with wool linings because it was cold in October. We never owned jackets before. On our return to Cofradía we walked around proudly with our new acquisitions and thought we were the coolest dudes in town."

José Velasco remained in Arizona, invisible to his children, inaccessible to his wife with only intermittent letters containing modest remittances to help with household expenses.

24

His father's absence prompted Antonio to recall: "At the age of seven or eight two or three years seems like a long time. And every two or three years after my father came home, my mother would have a baby. It confused me. I thought the father had to remain for the baby to be born. I tried to figure out who took his place. There was no one. When he came home I became jealous because he took my mother away from me."

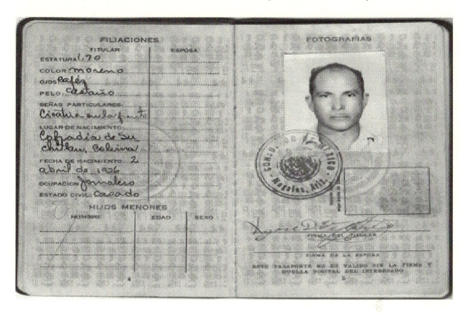

José Velasco Passport. Issued 1962 at Nogales, Arizona Port of Entry October 1962. (Velasco Family Archive)

With Antonio's father out of his life for extended periods he lacked a close male role model. Attachment to his mother provided nurture, love of learning, and a healing talent that gave him stability in an insecure world.

Antonio reflected about the influence of geography on his temperament. "Living in the foothills of the volcano I had a good sense for who I was. Lava flowed down the mountain almost on a daily basis. A little higher and to the north rises an extinct volcano covered in snow from February through May. The volcano is visible from anywhere in the region, so I always knew my place was south of the mountain. The mountains were a barrier between my father and me. In my mind, beyond the volcano was a nebulous area of foggy lakes that represented a vast unknown I couldn't picture."

The government built a stucco and concrete two-room school in the village constructed for purpose and not as elegant architecture. Antonio attended grades one to three. Across the hall David attended a class for grades four to six.

Decades later the village repurposed the school as a community center catering to the needs of modern society reflected in a sign hanging on the center's fence: "*Neuróticos Anónimos: Para de Sufrir Miedos, Depresión, Angustia, Celos, Ansiedad, Soledad, etc...*" (Neurotics Anonymous for those suffering Fear, Depression, Grief, Anxiety, Loneliness). Provincial villages rarely recognized those maladies in 1960.

Antonio had a voracious appetite for learning. He devoured David's science and math books. During the summer and on weekends Antonio hiked through the forest learning about and collecting herbs with his mother.

Teresa was born in Hacienda Nogueras eight miles south of Cofradía de Suchitlán after her mother Rosario was raped by Don Aureliano Rangel a wealthy rancher descended from Portuguese settlers who ran his domain as a feudal lord. [20]

Antonio Velasco recalled a family story about his grandmother: "As an unwed mother Rosario had few choices in the small village. She left my mother behind in the hacienda with her grandmother and married Cirilo Rubio a career soldier in the Mexican Army.

26

"My mother learned about herbs from her hard-working, strict grandmother, Antonia, who knew the art of making medicine from plants. After my mother married José Velasco from Cofradía de Suchitlán at the age of fourteen she became a self-taught student. She didn't have access to a lot of reading material but what she read she remembered. My mother took advantage of classes offered by the government. One of those classes trained her as a nurse's aide, where she was taught how to give injections and inoculations."

The Mexican Department of Health provided Teresa with a steady income. It sent nurses into the highlands to teach current health practices. Teresa dutifully placed the largess received along with remittances from her absent husband in a *guardadito*, [21] a clay pot buried behind the house.

Teresa treated men, women and children with balms, salves, and tonics to sooth pain, stomachaches, earaches and joints swollen from working sunrise to sunset. On a good day her patients paid with cash. Otherwise she received eggs, chickens, bread or milk. Teresa bartered health care services for sandals and shoes, shirts, jackets, trousers or dresses for herself and Meyo.

After graduating from Residency with a sub-specialty in obstetrics Antonio related how his mother assisted in two challenging births. "One time she was called to help with a breech presentation. Somehow she intuited that the baby would turn if they made the situation weightless. She ordered four strong men to stretch out a blanket and placed the pregnant woman in the center. They literally tossed her up and down as if on a trampoline. The baby turned and was delivered without a problem. As a physician I don't know if it happened because the woman relaxed or if she concentrated more on her safety and forgot the pain of delivery. I never heard of anyone doing something like that before or after.

"Another instance happened when a neighbor had a difficult delivery. She had been in the end-stage of labor for five hours and was out of control and wouldn't or couldn't push any more. My mother ordered the midwife and two others to hold her down. My mother poured olive oil into the pregnant woman's mouth and she retched—in effect pushing down. The baby was born. I have no idea where she came up with that notion, but it worked."

The Velasco clan made up almost sixty percent of Cofradía's population. Paternal grandparents, aunts, uncles and multitudes of cousins watched out for one another in the tight-knit confines of the village. For Antonio's immediate family Teresa was the only parent the children knew intimately.

Life without José Velasco seemed the norm therefore when he came home on infrequent visits it disturbed the stability provided by Teresa. His alcoholic binges and visceral need for approval created a degree of chaos.

Antonio's recollection of family life in Cofradía did not include his father. He had other, more pastoral, peaceful memories. His paternal grandmother Escolástica Chávez Castellanos, whom everyone called *Mamá* Nico, was a caring woman with a delightful sense of humor.

"She lived in her kitchen, a room made of sticks and mud walls with a tarpaper roof. My grandmother was always making fresh tortillas in front of her *pretil*, a bench covered with gray paste made from ashes and a little lime... I would ask her if there were any beans left. When she answered 'no' I would ask her '¿ni sal?' ("Not even any salt?"). She would smile and say '¡*Sal, sí mi hijo!*' ("Salt, yes my son"). She would then pick up the next tortilla and place thick grains of sea salt inside, roll it tightly and make little ears in the top. It was delicious." Antonio's paternal grandfather was the polar opposite.

Although he never witnessed the dark side of Jesús Velasco Ávalos, stories ran rampant about his alcoholism and uncontrollable temper.

"Family members told me he would get drunk with his friends, ride his horse into my grandmother's bedroom, pull her out by her hair and demand she cook them a meal," related Antonio. "During his rampages he would summon my father and make him kneel before him. Then he beat him with a thick piece of wood. After the beating my father couldn't get out of bed for days. My grandmother would plead for him and she would be beaten as well."

The frightening image of savage cruelty done without remorse did not equate with Antonio's relationship with Jesús Velasco. His grandfather treated all his grandchildren with kindness if not overt warmth. Antonio attempted to understand both sides of his grandfather's impulsive nature. He used violence as a cudgel to demonstrate power over adults who were under his patronage. On the other hand he craved the attention of children who were no threat. The lesson his grandfather taught him unknowingly was never act harshly or violently against anyone. That creed influenced the way he treated his wife, his children and eventually individuals who came to him for care.

Antonio's closest allies were his cousin Guadalupe whom everyone called Lupio and Florencio known by the nickname Lencho. Lencho was two years older than Antonio and the youngest of his father's twelve siblings therefore Antonio's uncle. Lencho lived with Mamá Nico and Jesús.

At the peril of receiving a scolding or whipping, the boys often skipped school and climbed into the mountains on adventurous hikes. Foothills rose forty-five hundred feet to the northeast. They trekked under a giant canopy of black walnut, ash and wild coffee trees where Green Iguanas as long as five feet from nose to tail hid in the foliage.

The boys fished in ponds formed by creeks surging into a gorge overgrown with giant ferns and wild orchids. Their favorite spot was a shallow pond on top of a mountain replenished constantly by rain and warmed by the sun.

The lush landscape fertilized by lava flows over thousands of years yielded a bounty of medicinal herbs. Seasons determined the rhythm of life in Antonio's world. His mother cared deeply for him. With a father absent for years at time the only image he conjured was based on his friends' fathers. José loomed large not only as a person but with an outsized personality.

Antonio later said: "Even my mother seemed big when I was seven years old."

The image imploded when José stepped off an old bus in Cofradía in the late summer of 1961. The stocky man with a weathered face wore faded jeans and a denim work shirt. His new Stetson, cowboy boots and white jacket were a concession to his status as a visitor from *El Norte* to his extended family in the village.

"When he came home he drank with friends," recalled Antonio. "They would come to our house and party for two or three weeks. Everyone had a good time. My mother joined the other women and did all the cooking. My father hired the local band and there was dancing. During those times he was good to us and smiled. After he sobered up he became withdrawn and said very little."

A meal for twenty or thirty people remained etched as a memory of his mother's resourcefulness and sense of humor.

"My mother was upset that she had to feed so many people. My father ordered her to make chicken. It would have decimated our small flock of hens that provided us with eggs we sold. Mama had to improvise. After the feast everyone exclaimed it was the best chicken they ever had and asked for the recipe. 'Skin an iguana and roast it' she told the shocked guests."

José's inclination to prove his generosity led to a dramatic incident that transformed the life of his family. He loaned five hundred pesos to a neighbor. After several weeks of partying the time came to travel back to Arizona. He asked for the return of his loan. The neighbor who had begged for help slammed the door in José's face.

José threatened to inform the village he had been deceived. The next day the ungrateful drunken neighbor staggered down the cobble stone street flourishing a large revolver. He shouted he would take revenge on José for calling him a cheat.

"My mother, brother and I looked through a small window of our stone house at a scene that could have been from a western movie. My father stood at one end of the street and our neighbor stood at the other waving a revolver in the air. My father hollered: 'I want the money now.' Suddenly the gun went off and my father, who was wearing his new white jacket, darted one way and the other and fell down. After running out of ammunition the shooter ran up the street shouting 'I just killed someone.' My father wasn't hurt but there were bullet holes in his jacket. He left town immediately. We stayed behind."

Chapter Three

San Luis Río Colorado

Jose hefted a small, battered suitcase and walked with Teresa to an old rust-flecked bus. No words passed between husband and wife. No tears flowed. He touched Teresa's hand in a futile gesture of affection and looked over her shoulder at the smoking mountain. Glowing red lava flowed slowly down its slopes into the valley with unerring regularity. The image of the fiery mountain and the gentle green rain-washed valley became indelibly fixed in José's memory.

Before he stepped aboard the bus Teresa pressed a roll of money retrieved from her *guardadito* in his hand. "Three hundred pesos. You'll need it," she said stoically.

The bus coughed to life. Black smoke belched from its exhaust as it trundled down the hill. José had gone and Teresa Velasco needed to take control of the situation. She used the one phone in the village *bodega* off the plaza to call Miguel, José's brother, a prison guard who worked in Guadalajara and lived in the city of Colima. She pleaded with him to collect her and the children out of fear their drunk neighbor would take revenge.

Antonio angrily stormed outside when she informed the children they had to leave the village. "I don't want to go.

I like things the way they are," he shouted.

"*Papa's* not coming back," said Teresa.

"He's always away. Even when he's here it's as if he's somewhere else. I don't know what difference it makes," Antonio snapped angrily.

"He's your father, that's the difference. He works up north so he can make enough money to support us. Be thankful."

"When are we leaving?" asked David.

"As soon as your Uncle Miguel gets here. In a day or two," said his mother.

"We can't leave so soon. I have to say goodbye to all my friends. What about school? Where will I go to school?" asked Antonio.

"You won't miss anything. There are schools in Colima," said Teresa.

Antonio ran to the edge of the village where Lupio, Atanasio and his younger brother Nano played soccer. He joined the game and kicked ferociously venting his anger on the ball. Afterward he sat on a splintered wood bench and buried his face in his hands.

"What's wrong?" asked Atanasio.

"We're moving away," cried Antonio.

"Because of what happened with your father?" asked Atanasio.

"I don't want to go. Who knows what will happen?" murmured Antonio.

Atanasio shook his hand. "You'll come back."

"You'll see. We'll meet again," said Lupio.

A few days later the morning sun glowed orange through clouds of steam belching from the volcano. Men and

34

women went to work on small farming plots or fed chickens and pigs or milked cows and goats as they did every day.

Teresa sat at the old familiar table where they ate their meals and the children did homework. Scars from years of wear were notes in a diary of hundreds of breakfasts, lunches and dinners. The table had absorbed laughter, quarrels, and long conversations about herbs, animals, the volcano, family history and a future tied to the village and highlands of Mexico.

Soft rain pattered on the clay tile roof. The luxuriant aroma of green ferns, sweet scent of flowers and banana plants permeated the air. Teresa consciously fixed the image of Cofradía, the valley and mountains in a corner of her mind.

Miguel arrived with a pickup truck into which they piled bits of furniture, kitchenware and clothing. Teresa, a young twenty-seven-year-old attractive, self-assured mother held three-year Teresa on her lap. Eight-year old Antonio, twelve-year old David and six-year old Meyo sat under a tarp in back holding fast to their belongings. They jounced down the muddy cobblestone road toward Miguel's home in Colima.

They had visited Colima and the beaches of Manzanillo, toured Guadalajara on brief vacations or spent time in Mexico City when their mother gave birth to Teresa. The children always knew they would return home.

Miguel roared out of the village hitting cobblestones and potholes at full speed. He pulled out his gun and fired it in the air shouting for all to hear that they were leaving and never returning.

"It wasn't violence of the moment. It was fear that a way of life was coming to an end," Antonio recalled. "The kids in the county seat of Colima had always been hostile toward my brother and me because we wore homemade outfits. They called us *Charros Montaperros*, dog-riding cowboys. We were going to live in their midst and the likelihood of returning to Cofradía seemed improbable."

They remained with Miguel, his wife Reyna and a multitude of cousins for several months during which time Antonio celebrated his ninth birthday. During a torrential rainstorm in mid-summer Teresa announced they were leaving: *"Nos vamos al norte."* ("We're northbound.") They sold what little they had. With only their suitcases they left Colima on the *Omnibus de Mexico* for the short ride to Guadalajara.

The bus thumped over a rocky, unpaved road. A torrent of rain turned the road into a slick muddy river. The rain halted and the sun came out when they reached the city. David helped an elderly woman off the bus. She patted his curly red hair.

"I congratulate you," she said to Teresa. "Your children are very kind."

Teresa accepted the compliment proudly. "My children are my greatest blessing."

She called to them while they waited for the northbound bus. "I have a surprise for all of you. Very soon we're going to have a baby in the family.

"Where is it coming from?" asked little Teresa.

"From God. The baby's going to be our very own," said their mother. "Is it going to a boy or girl?" asked Antonio.

"It doesn't make any difference. We will love the baby just like I love all of you."

*San Luis Rio Colorado, Mexico, 1964. L to R: Teresa (6), Meyo
(9), Antonio (11). (Velasco Family Archive)*

They changed buses for the trip to the border town
of San Luis Rio Colorado 1300 miles away. For a nine-year
old the trip represented an odyssey to a fabled land existing
behind a magic curtain. The small cinema in Colima often
played American movies depicting happy children, beautiful
women and handsome men living in elegant homes. On the
open plains of the west John Wayne swaggered through a
landscape of mesas, red buttes, and towering mountains
stoically helping those who could not help themselves.

Trepidation mixed with excitement overcame Antonio
when the bus roared to life. Passengers scrambled aboard
carrying battered suitcases, packages, and sacks filled with
food for the long journey. A tall, thin man with a grizzled

face, dark, brooding eyes and a sweeping black mustache sat in an aisle seat. Patched jeans had seen better days. He pulled a stained Stetson over his eyes.

An old woman dressed in black with a black lace mantilla over her head hobbled up the steps of the bus with the assistance of a gnarled ebony cane. The driver offered to help. She pushed his hands away and sat directly behind him.

On the tedious drive Antonio recalled that after an hour imaginations began to roam. The brothers invented stories about their fellow passengers.

"I bet the man with the mustache is a bandit. He's going to meet his gang and rob a bank," whispered David.

"Maybe we can get a reward for stopping the robbery," said Antonio. "We'll get a million pesos and never have to work a day in our lives."

"Or the bandits could line us up against a wall and kill us," David said.

Antonio sat up straight. "We'll die with honor."

The boys shook hands. "With honor," they said at the same time.

Antonio leaned over the back of his seat. "Meyo, you see that old lady?" He pointed at the black clad woman with the cane.

She peered down the aisle. "What about her?"

"She's a witch. She steals little girls like you and cooks them for dinner," he said in a low, frightening voice.

"Mama, Tonio's scaring us. Tell him to stop," yelled Meyo.

"What are you doing?" Teresa demanded

"He said the lady's a witch," Meyo whispered.

"There's no such thing." She pulled a leather belt from her purse. "Tonio, stop making up stories or else you'll feel this against your backside."

"We're tired of looking out the window at nothing," Antonio replied.

Thunder cracked across the sky. Rain pounded the bus as it climbed a mountain highway skirting the edge of a steep cliff. Lightning illuminated rusted, twisted skeletons of buses, trucks and automobiles buried halfway in a muddy pool at the bottom of a ravine.

David poked Antonio in the ribs and pointed at the wreckage. "That doesn't look like nothing." He strode to the front of the bus.

"You're not allowed up here. Get back where you belong," the driver bellowed at him.

"Keep your eyes on the road or we'll end up like those other buses," shouted David.

"You do the sitting and let me drive."

"What happened in the canyon?" David asked.

"Drivers try to get from one stop to the next on time. They have a saying: 'Better dead than late.' Sometimes they get careless."

"What about you?"

"I have a wife and children. What use would I be to them if I were dead," answered the driver. "Get back in your seat."

David slipped next to his brother. "We could be next."

"That's scary," said Antonio.

"Just think how the people felt in those buses."

"I don't want to think about it. I just want to go back home," sighed Antonio.

"Forget about Cofradía. It's not our home any longer."

David's fatalistic statement threw an immense cloak of distress around Antonio. The mountains rising above Cofradía, the dense forest and sun-dappled creeks and pools became a world that faded with every mile.

The steady chug of the engine and thump of wheels lulled Antonio to sleep. He envisioned his father riding a horse with a silver-lined saddle. Jose dressed in an embroidered shirt, jeans and handsome cowboy hat. Antonio ran toward him. Clouds of dust obscured the idyllic picture. They lifted and his father's image vanished.

The squeal of brakes jolted him awake. They had passed through the storm and drove into a farm town at the convergence of two rivers. The bus parked near a plaza surrounded by sugarcane, tobacco fields, lemon and orange orchards that permeated the air with the sweet odor of citrus.

Antonio and David ran into the plaza. Meyo and little Teresa stayed close to their mother. Men and women strolled in the square during the brief period between rainstorms. Trumpets and violins filled the air with familiar songs. Antonio's feelings of loss faded until he wearily climbed aboard the bus. Gears clashed and the engine revved with a dull knocking noise.

The bus traveled west on a downward slope through verdant farmlands, past villages and small towns with ubiquitous church spires towering over humble homes. The rural landscape merged into an urban barrio of tin-roofed huts edging up to grim manufacturing facilities and warehouses.

Further west, the city took on the role of tourist mecca with attractive hotels bordering the Pacific Ocean. Morning

40

sunlight danced across crystal blue waves lapping up on white, sandy beaches of Mazatlán.

A lighthouse painted with a spiraling red stripe stood atop a tall outcropping of granite that dropped precipitously into the sea. Young men clad in bathing suits stood on the edge of the cliff, waved to the beach crowd and leaped forty-five feet into rampaging, shallow water.

"They must be crazy," David shouted.

"Tourists pay divers to jump off the rock. They do it as long as people are willing to give them money," said Teresa.

"No one could pay me enough. They can die or be crippled for life," exclaimed Antonio.

"They need money to pay for food and keep a roof over their heads, Tonio. Who are we to judge?" asked his mother.

The bus rolled out of Mazatlan and turned inland stopping every hour at small settlements and hamlets. Faces of passengers changed the closer they came to the American border.

On the next to the last day of their journey rough looking men wearing tattered jeans and old scuffed boots climbed aboard. When the children made noise they glared at them with dark eyes under the brims of sweat-stained caps and cowboy hats.

"They're a gang of revolutionaries led by a man who's the great-grandson of Miguel Hidalgo, general of the Mexican army," Antonio whispered to David.

"Get your story straight. Hidalgo was a priest. He couldn't have children," said David.

Little Teresa yanked at her mother's skirt and whispered to her. Teresa walked to the driver.

"Please sit down, *señora*. You're not allowed up here," he ordered.

"If you don't want to wash out the inside of your bus you better pull over or my daughter's going to have a very big accident," she said.

In his rearview mirror he saw Little Teresa bouncing anxiously on the seat. "Five minutes," he sighed with resignation.

Meyo and little Teresa followed by everyone else on the bus rushed into a grove of trees. A few minutes later they emerged with relieved smiles on their faces.

The green hills and mountains of the Mexican highlands slowly gave way to the dry, forbidding Sonoran Desert.[22] Tall Saguaro cactus raised prickly arms to the bright blue sky. Fields of sharp-thorned Cholla turned brittle in the harsh arid environment. Black mesquite twisted against sand and boulders. Mild nighttime temperatures rose rapidly through the day scorching the earth with triple digits. Oven-hot air gusted through open windows caking passengers with fine grit blowing off the desert.

On the morning of the fourth day they rolled into the sunbaked town of San Luis Rio Colorado[23] on the northern frontier of Mexico. David made a phone call to his father from the border checkpoint announcing their arrival.

"He [José] didn't know we were coming," Antonio remembered David announcing when he returned to the bus terminal.

His father arrived in an old car. Disgruntled and annoyed at the unexpected arrival of his wife and children, he abruptly dropped them off at a friend's house.

"I was not happy meeting my father on the border. I

42

didn't know him. Everyone in Cofradía called him Dolores but here he was known as José. He insisted we call him Papá José," Antonio reminisced years later.

Chapter Four

A Hint of Sand

Teresa exploded with indignation at the sight of a cinder block cabin with a bare dirt floor, no water and no electricity. Wind-whipped sand piled against walls. Tumbleweed bounced erratically along unpaved streets. Disabled automobiles and trucks on blocks or without engines scattered among jerrybuilt shanties on plots of land occupied by lizards and scorpions.

"We travel four days and a hut waits for us because you had to escape from Cofradía?" she angrily asked.

"It's all I can afford," he replied. "What could I do?"

"Saved your money instead of drinking it. I will not have our children living in a miserable shack. The least we can do is buy mattresses, a table and chairs, a rug to cover the dirt floor and a barbecue for cooking," ordered Teresa.

The family drove out of the barrio into a town of adobe and brick homes. Teresa ordered José to stop the car in front of *Mueblería El Campesino,* a furniture store under the arcade of Hotel Río Colorado.

"Here's where we're buying what we need," said Teresa.

"We don't have enough money," José said.

"Do you have any other ideas?" Teresa asked without hope.

"Trust me. You'll have your mattresses." José stepped on the gas.

44

He drove north to the twin towers of Immaculate Conception Catholic Church on Avenida Manuel Hidalgo. A priest met them inside the beautiful vaulted sanctuary and escorted them to a storeroom stacked with beds, tables, chairs and rugs. Under a blanket in one corner they found an unrefrigerated icebox that had been there since the church began collecting goods for indigent families. A barbecue with a rusted grill stood in another corner.

"We'll be back tomorrow. I have a friend with a truck," José told the priest.

The Father said it wasn't necessary. The church would deliver whatever they picked out. "We want your children to know we care."

Two hours later the church truck arrived at the cinder block house and unloaded two beds with mattresses, a table and chairs, a small threadbare rug, the old icebox, and the barbecue. After settling his wife and children in the house, José declared he had no intention of remaining in San Luis Rio Colorado. He lived with *compadres* across the border in San Luis, Arizona.

Teresa adamantly ordered him to pay attention to his duties as a husband and father. She recounted the hardships his family encountered for years in Cofradía. In contrast to other *braceros* who visited their families once or twice every year, he made sporadic trips home after a two or three year hiatus. If he didn't need to show off how much money he made and loan it to a parasite, Teresa would never have been forced to leave home.

José surrendered for a brief period. As time passed he arrived later and later after spending time drinking in a bar across from the border checkpoint.

His father's absence did not bother Antonio who enjoyed the company of the mother. She had been the sole caretaker most of his life. Teresa, on the other hand, worried that José would squander his earnings on drinking binges. She sent the reluctant boys across the border to the saloon to remind their father to return home.

The sight of his children acting as babysitters amused his *compadres;* it did not amuse José who relented to David and Antonio's pleas. Teresa and José accommodated each other. Underneath he smoldered with resentment that his wife and children disrupted his routine.

Bigotry and bias heavily freighted relations between Anglo and Hispanic populations in Yuma where José worked. A story in the local newspaper headlined derisively "51 Wet Mexicans" exemplified the Anglo point of view. It reported an immigration raid on "Mexican immigrants who had entered the country illegally..."[24] Necessity from major agriculture holdings that needed farm workers shunted aside most immigration problems.

San Luis Rio Colorado's population was Hispanic and mostly transient. Unfortunately it also manifested internecine intolerance. Urban Mexicans rarely mixed with those who came from small agrarian villages and towns.

"I felt I was in an alien world. Spanish spoken in San Luis had different words and accents. I couldn't fit in. I was alone," recounted Antonio.

School became his major priority. Although Antonio had difficulty making friends, he excelled in class. He spent most of his time studying, reading, and watching over his sisters. His brother David had an opportunity to attend The Commercial Industrial Technical Academy in San Luis established by the Mexican government. The tuition free academy trained bookkeepers and accountants for civil service positions, and banks. David passed the stringent examination with stellar scores and gained admittance.

The torrid days of summer slowly gave way to fall and winter. By November temperatures dropped to the mid-seventies and kept falling. Sporadic rainstorms showered the barren desert landscape. It burst forth with vivid pink cactus roses, white desert lilies, brilliant yellow Mexican sunflowers, and scarlet *ocotillo*.

Owls emerged from nests burrowed in towering Saguaro cactus. Birds flitted among brightly colored flowers. Long eared jackrabbits skittered from bush to bush nibbling at new green vegetation. Foxes stealthily tracked the jackrabbits and ground squirrels. In the early morning bobcats roamed the desert searching for prey. As if echoing the renewal of the desert, Teresa gave birth to her third daughter, Cecilia in 1963. Antonio was ten-years old.

San Luis Rio Colorado held a winter festival celebrating the Sonora Desert's rebirth. It was a high point for Antonio and his siblings. Stalls selling sweet corn tamales, fried *churros* coated with sugar and Native American wares populated the midway. It was one of the few times the boys felt close to their father who let down his guard.

José rode with them on the Ferris wheel and roller coaster and played carnival games. The family attended performances by Mariachi bands. Children from public and church schools presented traditional Mexican dances. Local Yaqui Indians wearing decorated deer heads and rattles carved from deer hooves demonstrated their venerable dance in tribute to animals that died to feed their tribe.

Joy of the moment brought the family together. Teresa and José purchased tamales, enchiladas, beans, rice and tortillas. They sat at a picnic table near the end of the midway when a woman sauntered up and leaned against a post as if posing for a photographer.

"Looks as if you're having a good time, José," she said sarcastically.

"Who are you?" Teresa demanded.

"A friend of José. Who are you?" she answered.

José's face turned red. He stood abruptly and swiftly walked away.

"Don't think you can get away lying to me José Velasco," she shouted.

Teresa, fire in her eyes, handed Cecilia to Antonio. She grabbed the woman's arm.

"You better talk to me. I'm José's wife," snapped Teresa.

"You tell your husband that I need a loan. And he better give me the money," she said pulling away from Teresa. "He's no angel."

"What are you talking about?" Teresa insisted.

"Hasn't he told you? Ever since he came to Yuma we've been living together."

"My mother who was passionately non-violent looked the woman up and down and told her she was in charge of the money," recalled Antonio. "She pulled a large switchblade knife from her purse that she carried to cut vegetables or fruit when we were on picnics and said, 'Let me give you the money.' The frightened woman fled. My father never saw her again. It was the first and last time my mother acted counter to her personality."

The episode did not culminate in a tragic ending. José mended his ways and promised he would never stray again. Teresa forgave him but did not forget. Her goal, as always, said Antonio, was to protect her children and make sure they had at least one parent with whom they could share their dreams.

Antonio rose to the top percentile in math, science and language at school. He made friends with classmates at the same educational level who did not discriminate against his rural background.

Teachers discussed the new relationship with Mexico inaugurated by the young President of the United States John F. Kennedy who visited Mexico in 1962 with First Lady Jacqueline Kennedy. She addressed the gathering in Spanish endearing her and the president to the people. His speech to the citizens of Mexico pushed forward Franklin Delano Roosevelt's Good Neighbor Policy.

"Our nations share more than 2,000 miles of a peaceful frontier. More than three million of my own countrymen are of Mexican descent," stated Kennedy. "We share a common history and a common faith in democracy... We are both children of revolution. The Mexican revolution and the American Revolution had in common a passion for the expansion of social justice, economic opportunity, national independence and personal freedom. And today we struggle to complete the work which our revolutionary ancestors began — to carry forward a hemisphere-wide *Alianza para el Progresso* to win a better and more abundant life for all the people of the Americas."[25]

The hopes and dreams of millions of Americans and Mexicans crashed on Friday, November 22, 1963. A clerk rushed into Antonio's third grade class a few minutes after one o'clock and whispered to the teacher. She looked shocked and announced the cancellation of all classes for the rest of the day.

Someone held up a transistor radio for all to hear: *"From Dallas, Texas, the flash apparently official, President Kennedy died at one pm Central Standard Time, two pm Eastern Standard Time, some thirty-eight minutes ago."*

"A commotion broke out in the neighborhood as the radio gave the news," recalled Antonio. "Men and women came out of their homes and talked to their neighbors. People cried."

Vice-President Lyndon Johnson was sworn in as President of the United States and presided over an increasingly tense period during which the Vietnam War intensified. Mexico remained neutral during the conflict.

Three years after settling in San Luis David, fifteen, prepared to graduate from the academy. His dream came to a halt on August 23, 1964 when José received permission to bring his family across the border into the United States. He demanded that David work to support the family. David rebelled. His protest had no impact. The devastating blow to his desire for higher education took a heavy toll on the boy.

"He was top of his class. He could have gone to high school and college. His personality changed from robust, sociable and popular," said Antonio. "He rarely worked in the fields because he attended the academy. Suddenly he went from academia to farm labor. David became depressed and lost weight. He had no experience working in orchards, but my father expected all of us to work as he worked. My father's philosophy was steadfast. If you work hard you will survive."

50

José ignored the trauma dealt his eldest son. He had set in motion a plan to obtain permission to bring his family into the United States. They traveled to Nogales, Arizona[26] the nearest immigration center. Two weeks later they received their final papers, a Family Passport with a photo of Teresa and her five children, David, fifteen, Antonio, eleven, Meyo (Remedios), nine, Teresa, four, and Cecelia, ten months. It was signed Teresa Ramirez, date of birth March 6, 1934 with the official stamp at the entry point "Consulado de Mexico— Nogales, Ariz." From Nogales they traveled 314 miles east to the small town of Somerton, Arizona[27] between San Luis Rio Colorado and Yuma.

David grudgingly trekked to a lemon ranch with his father and worked until the rancher discovered he was fifteen years old. Arizona state law prohibited anyone under sixteen from working during the school year. José quit his job and went to work for another rancher who wanted him to supervise irrigation. He ordered David to lie about his age. The trauma and disappointment remained with his eldest son for decades.

The difference between living in San Luis Rio Colorado and Somerton made a deep impression on Antonio. "Movies I saw at the Cine Royal in San Luis made America look as if there was a carnival every day. Everyone had toys and candy and automobiles. I was coming to the land of opportunity," Antonio reported.

They rented an apartment in a courtyard building that seemed as if it emerged from a fairy tale. Trees shaded a large garden. Grass and flowers grew in the center of the court. The apartment had running water, a bathroom, and electricity.

Antonio's entry into school in Somerton was not what he expected. "I had no English speaking, reading or writing skills. The school placed me and most new immigrants in a class for what they considered mentally challenged children. I knew in my heart it would always be an uphill battle," said Antonio.

He languished in the remedial track until his teacher reviewed Antonio's math competency scores. She transferred him to a mainstream fourth-grade class. Jesse, the leader of a group of Mexican American boys immediately saw the bright, intelligent newcomer as someone with whom he had an affinity. He undertook the task of helping Antonio improve his English. Within a short time his language skills progressed.

Recognition of his innate talent in math and science and having friends with whom he shared both a common heritage and love of education provided Antonio with a new sense of purpose.

Tranquilino (Kili) Rendón, Jr., the son of José's co-worker Tranquilino Rendón, and Antonio became close friends at Somerton Elementary. They spent time with Jesse and the other boys playing basketball and soccer in the park. The boys fished with handmade rods in Somerton Canal that ran from the Colorado River south to farms surrounding the town. A few months later Kili's father moved his family to Greenfield, California where harvests were plentiful, and growers offered better wages for qualified farm workers.

Life in the small Arizona town moved at a leisurely pace. Movies Antonio played in his dreams came alive. He lived in an apartment far different from the small stone house in Cofradía de Suchitlán and the dirt floor cabin to which his family had been relegated in San Luis Rio Colorado. The town had parks, shops, restaurants and the mission-style Immaculate Heart of Mary Catholic Church where they attended mass every Sunday.

After mass Antonio walked nine-year old Meyo and five-year old Teresa to a tree shaded park near the apartment. The family had reached a new Eden. Unfortunately this Eden had its own snake. Two sisters from Antonio's school demanded Meyo and Teresa get off the swings so they could use them.

"Stay where you are," Antonio ordered his sisters. Folding his arms defiantly across his chest, he turned to the girls. "We got here a few minutes ago. You have to wait your turn.

"This is our park and our swings. You don't belong here. Go back to Mexico," one of the sisters yelled.

"You'll have to make us leave," said Antonio.

Angry and frustrated the girls ran home and brought back their brother. "I remember his name to this day," reminisced Antonio. "Joe was the school bully, a year older and a head taller than me."

"Get the hell out of here. The swings are for Americans not little wetbacks like you and your sisters," Joe smirked.

Furious at the assault on his family Antonio impetuously butted his head into the bigger boy's stomach. Joe smashed his fist into Antonio's cheek slamming him to the ground. Blood dripped from his nose and one of his eyes swelled shut. Before returning home bruised and battered, he made his sisters promise not to tell their mother what happened.

His mother gasped at the sight of Antonio's black-and-blue eye and bloody nose. He told her he fell off a wall in the park. Even though he lost the battle he apparently won the war. He never had another confrontation with the bully.

David knew the real story. As a reward for his brother's defense of their sisters he repaired a bicycle rescued from a salvage yard and gave it to Antonio so he could join his friends on bike rides.

Before the end of the school year in the spring of 1965 one of the boys who befriended Antonio broke into tears. His mother planned to leave Somerton for Los Angeles. It reminded Antonio of the day he learned his mother planned to leave Cofradía. Jesse, Antonio, and the others pooled their meager change and exchanged it for a crisp new five-dollar bill. They gave it to their departing friend as a gift.

In May the weather turned from mild spring to the searing heat of desert summer. Antonio picked green onions on a farm at the edge of town. Teresa and David joined José in the Yuma orchards while Meyo remained home to care for little Teresa.

Every morning Antonio trudged through fields pulling onions out of the earth, carefully brushing sand off each bulb and binding bunches with rubber bands. The farmer waited under a large umbrella, a jug of ice water beside him, examining the freshly picked produce. If he spotted the slightest hint of sand on the onions a thunder of anger erupted, and he withheld wages from farm hands.

Resentment festered under Antonio's skin at the injustice against men, women and children who toiled in the broiling sun for hours, backs bent, enduring excruciating pain under incredibly harsh conditions. It was another notch carved in his memory; a reminder he had to do something else with his life.

José's *compadres* were leaving for California to take advantage of long harvest seasons and the opportunity to earn more money. Without consulting Teresa he abruptly announced they were moving to the Salinas Valley for the summer harvest.

David complained bitterly that his father destroyed his dream of working in a bank and now wanted to force him to go to a strange land. Antonio resented José for uprooting him from a familiar place. The brothers' arguments fell on deaf ears. They gave up their apartment and packed their car with a few belongings.

Antonio begged his father to take the bicycle David bought for him.

"There's no room for your bicycle. You have to leave it behind," said José.

"Tie it to the roof," Antonio suggested.

"And when it falls off and hits another car who's going to pay? It's not going with us," José said with finality.

Antonio rode his bicycle to Immaculate Heart Church. "Give it to a kid who really wants it," Antonio said to the priest.

The Velascos drove west on Interstate 8 through Yuma. They crossed a bridge spanning the sluggish, murky Colorado River into California. Waving fields of alfalfa and melons ripening on vines in the broiling hot Imperial Valley sucked up life-giving water.

An invisible barrier of intense heat rose out of the brutal hostile dry Colorado Desert. Black and gray creosote scrub, yucca and spiny, olive-green saltbush pushed against sand dunes. The black asphalt ribbon of highway wavered and quivered under a searing sun.

Farther west chaparral covered mountains loomed closer and closer. Green covered hills were a welcome sight after the dreary scorched desert landscape. José pulled the car to a turnoff beneath a sign that read 'Entering Cleveland National Forest'. Teresa prepared a meal of rice and beans, bananas and apples with a package of store-bought tortillas. Birds chattered in the branches of an oak tree. Squirrels scampered up and down its rough bark pausing to eat acorns while warily watching invaders on their home turf.

The temperature dropped precipitously as the sun lowered in the west. The children huddled on the back seat. José and Teresa burrowed beneath a blanket in front. In the morning they began the long ascent over the mountain range. Seventeen hundred feet above sea level they drove through the small town of Alpine with its old west wood storefronts and houses. Antonio expected to see his favorite western heroes stride along the boardwalks, spurs ringing with every step. The sight of tourists in shorts and Hawaiian shirts wiped out his expectations.

On the downgrade past Alpine tree-covered mountains gave way to dusty, brown hills sparsely dotted with oak and acacia trees. José scanned cars at service stations until he saw another farm worker. They engaged in lengthy conversations that ended with handshakes. Every time he returned to the car José said the same thing: "There's plenty of work where we're going."

He drove up the coast of California skirting towns and cities perched above white beaches. While still dark they sped north into the crowded highways of Los Angeles where a gray pall hung over the sprawling city.

A few miles north they climbed curving Highway 99, "The Grapevine," to three thousand feet above haze obscuring Los Angeles. They continued past a vast network of farms and feedlots milling with hundreds of head of cattle. Flames from tall oil refinery stacks flared into the Bakersfield atmosphere. Giant oil tankers with massive wheels thundered past their car.

The highway paralleled the Salinas River through a pass in Los Padres National Forest and entered the fertile Salinas Valley[28] where long lines of straw-hatted men, women and children bobbed up and down mechanically between rows.

Chapter Five

The American Dream

The Velascos joined a crew with Tranquilino Rendón and his son Kili in a labor camp of old wood cabins beneath a stand of eucalyptus trees. Workers were packed in trucks that transported them to ranches glistening with bright red tomatoes growing on staked vines extending miles in every direction. Early morning fog lifted and temperatures soared blasting fields with intense heat.

Warned that bruised fruit would result in withheld wages, the same threat Antonio received picking green onions in Somerton, he and Meyo approached the job with deep apprehension. Their father immediately demonstrated to Antonio and Meyo how to efficiently and safely pick tomatoes off the vine with an economic twist.

After thirty minutes Antonio's back froze, his wrists ached, and his fingers became numb. He straightened up and José warned him the pain would worsen when he bent down again. No one rested. The only water available flowed through irrigation canals. Meyo threw up. Antonio's hands swelled.

Two weeks later they experienced severe back cramps, spasms and aching legs from chopping and thinning rows of lettuce hour after hour with short-handled hoes forcing them to remain bent over for long hours.

They picked grapes in Fresno where temperatures soared into triple digits. Field managers watched every bunch rolling down conveyor belts. Men, women, and children once more lived in constant fear minor infractions would result in severe financial penalties.

The migrant farmworker trail traveled northwest to the cherry orchards of Morgan Hill a town that straddled northbound Highway 101. The Velascos climbed up with sacks over their shoulders on long ladders into the trees. It was a welcome respite from the torment of constantly stooping over. Another advantage for the children is that ranchers didn't mind if workers sampled cherries.

Antonio questioned his father about the wispy coat of white on the fruit. "Don't worry," he reassured him. "If it were dangerous the farmers would warn us." They wiped off the coating and popped cherries in their mouths.

That night Antonio and Meyo doubled over in pain throwing up violently. Teresa collected plants from the countryside and boiled a tonic for her children. By morning they felt strong enough to continue working.

"One of the worst episodes occurred when we picked strawberries in Salinas," Antonio reminisced. "Crops were thickly sprayed, and we could see white residue and smell chemicals. But we were children and ate as many strawberries as we could while working. At the end of the day many of us fell ill with headaches and diarrhea. At the time I had no idea what caused it, but I did know it made me sick."

Antonio and Meyo returned to work pulling carrots on Soledad farms. At each ranch José proudly told foremen that his sons and daughter worked harder than any man or woman in the field. With their father's instructions, they doubled their output.

Teresa carefully wrote in a notebook every dollar earned. José traded in his old station wagon for a used panel truck. David passed his automobile license test and took over most of the driving.

Farmworkers flocked to the broccoli harvest south of Salinas in the Central Valley town of Greenfield[29] between the Gabilan Range to the east of the Salinas Valley and the Diablo Range on California's Central Coast near the rugged Santa Lucia mountains.

"Working in broccoli affects your knees," recollected Antonio. "You're walking in water up to your waist. You spend the day cold and wet because the leaves are wet. You get pain in your knees because they're wet. A lot of people are afraid of broccoli because of the pain it causes in their knees."

It took hours for the suffering to ease. Antonio fell into a restless asleep knowing the moment the sun rose throbbing pain would return. A crackling explosion roared across the night sky. Orange and yellow flames engulfed a wood cabin where a family of farmworkers slept.

José ran to the hut and yanked open the door. Fire flared out driving him back. A small girl curled inside desperately clawing her way to the door. He scooped her up and ran to a water tank. Teresa and the other women in camp washed soot and grime from the girl's face as fire engines screamed down the highway.

Firefighters doused the flames leaving charred remnants on the ground. The shivering, shocked child's parents perished in the conflagration. Teresa wrapped a blanket around the girl's shoulders and comforted her with warm milk and biscuits.

Fire department paramedics treated the child and placed her in an ambulance under the care of Social Services.

José washed grime from his face and plunged blistered hands in a bucket of cold water. The incident balanced Antonio's resentment of his father's intransigent stoicism. Throughout the day, workers shook his father's bandaged hands thanking him for rescuing the child. He took the congratulations with silent patience and returned to work ignoring his burns.

"We're not staying here. I would rather sleep in the car than in one of these firetraps," Teresa firmly announced.

Her unyielding determination impacted José. That evening he arrived at the camp with Tranquilino Rendón who offered a spare room to the Velascos in his rented house in Greenfield.

Tranquilino's gentle disposition and affection toward his wife, Kili and their other children were new experiences for Antonio. Every night he prayed his father would show the smallest bit of tenderness. Those moments were usually limited to the amount of alcohol José consumed.

Doña Amparo Rendón and Teresa prepared meals for both families as well as substantial lunches for everyone to take into the field. *Doña* Amparo remained behind while José, Teresa, David, Antonio and Meyo rose early in the morning with Tranquilino and Kili and returned at sunset.

Time spent in the comfortable hospitable Rendón environment ended when José purchased an old trailer on a vacant lot near the highway. Cold, moist air seeped through warped metal seams and cracked windows. The children slept in narrow bunk beds. Meyo, little Teresa and Cecilia occupied the bottom tier. Antonio and David shared the top.

Lying in the narrow confines of the bunk Antonio dreamed he saw himself in a motion picture. "I fantasized the movie would fast forward to a future that would be better because it couldn't get worse. My new life would be more comfortable, more secure and I wouldn't be afraid of the next morning and hard work. In my dream I had a better lifestyle. At that age and without experience the future was hazy and nebulous and I couldn't pin it down."

The harvest dwindled by the end of August and they returned to Arizona. Their courtyard garden apartment had no vacancies. A labor camp located in the center of Somerton became their home for the rest of the year.

Antonio haunted the town library to improve his English after a summer of speaking Spanish. He would rather sit quietly and read books about plants that he did not painstakingly hoe and pick under the blistering sun. The mosquitoes and wasps he read about posed no physical threats.

He entered fifth grade on the first week of September. His teacher, Mrs. Sylvia F. Plotts, was known throughout the school as a no-nonsense stern but fair person. Years later Antonio fondly remembered her eyeglasses hanging from a chain around her neck. She usually wore a long-pleated skirt with a wide belt around her waist and piled her hair into a bun on top of her head.

Although demanding, Mrs. Plotts nevertheless treated each student as a unique individual. Every Friday she brought ice cream treats for her class. On one occasion a student sitting in the back row shattered Antonio's pleasant interlude.

Fourteen-year old Miguel attempted to steal Antonio's ice cream. Antonio pushed him away. Miguel twisted

62

Antonio's arm hard behind his back. He blacked out and fell in a heap to the floor. Mrs. Plotts came to his aid and ordered Miguel to the principal's office. From that time on Antonio occupied a desk in the front row. He flourished in her class and by December ranked top of his grade.

Over winter vacation the Velasco family spent Christmas in Mexico with their extended family in Colima. José insisted on remaining in Mexico forcing the children to miss the start of school in Somerton while José squandered the family's hard-earned wages on parties and liquor.

News filtered to Colima that the Bracero Program ended on New Year's Eve, 1964. Farm owners in the United States pressed the government to raise the quota of Mexican immigrants. Workers without Green Cards surreptitiously and illegally slipped across the border. Over time, it became apparent American laborers wanted little to do with backbreaking, tedious, low paying jobs on farms. Manufacturers of consumer goods and an aerospace industry that exploded exponentially paid higher wages than anyone could earn as a hired farm hand.

The demand for machinists, engineers and scientists became a priority. The end of the Bracero Program left farmers and their workers in a bind. Farmers lost a major source of labor and voiced their concerns about loss of income due to the inability to harvest crops.

Braceros without Green Cards were rounded up by authorities and sent back to their country of origin. Although they worked under brutal conditions for wages well below the national average the program had provided a source of income in the form of remittances to families left behind. José's possession of a Green Card allowed him to continue working as an irrigation supervisor in Yuma. He was king of the hill and let family and friends in Colima know about his good fortune. But he refused to pack up and move back to Arizona until he was ready.

Antonio pleaded with his mother that he and Meyo would suffer grave consequences as a result of missing school. Teresa forced Jose to relent. They arrived in Somerton three weeks after the spring school term began. Antonio went into hyper-speed. Determined not to fall behind he studied late into night. His English improved and he emerged once more with excellent grades.

A bright intelligent girl arrived in Somerton from Mexico in 1965 with her migrant farm worker family. With her aptitude for mathematics Elva García was admitted to Mrs. Plotts' fifth grade. Concerned for their daughter's safety, her parents forbade her to talk with boys. Elva was awed at Antonio's math proficiency.

She clearly recalled Antonio as "...very quiet and smart. He always received good grades in math and all his work. After fifth grade I didn't see him again for many years."

On the last day of school before summer break Mrs. Plotts announced her plan to leave Somerton. She requested Antonio remain behind after class. Mrs. Plotts planned to write a recommendation that he skip sixth grade and enter seventh because of his extraordinary academic ability.

"I remember being surprised by my teacher's faith in me," said Antonio years later. "In return for writing the note and in return for her compassion, I wanted to give her something to remember me. I gave her a Mexican *peso* I saved. Mrs. Plotts seemed overwhelmed by the gesture and for the first time I saw tears in her eyes and a smile on her face. She

64

smoothed out the wrinkled *peso* and wrote on it 'From Antonio to Mrs. Plotts' and placed it in her wallet."

Sylvia Plotts subsequently had a distinguished career in education as School Superintendent of Marion County, Iowa. The Sylvia Plotts Memorial Scholarship assists the education of Native American students.

Throughout the summer his teacher's confidence in him made the aches and pains Antonio endured on long, hot days in California trekking up and down rows of tomatoes, grapes, broccoli and lettuce worthwhile.

Advancing from fifth to seventh grade presented a major challenge. Almost every boy and girl excelled in English, math, and science. As the youngest in his class Antonio felt inadequate. Within a short time his intellect opened the door to acceptance from his classmates.

His high grades gave the family almost as much pleasure as the birth of Josefina. Born in a Yuma, Arizona hospital, Josefina was an American citizen. They hung the Stars and Stripes on the wall when Teresa and the baby came home. In the midst of the joyous party José abruptly declared they were returning to California.

Chapter Six

Friendship and Faith

During the long drive west in the summer of 1965, José spoke for the first time about his dream. "Crops grow almost year-round in the Salinas Valley. When there's no harvest we can do irrigation work, prune orchards, plant trees," José said as if he could see it happening. "Once we have enough money we're all going back to Mexico. I'll buy a ranch and have horses and cows and be respected."

Behind the bluster and drinking; beyond his worn wrinkled face, old denim shirt and faded jeans, José held tight to an image that kept him working year-after-year: the ever-present volcano and lush green valley of the Mexican Highlands.

José bought an old aluminum mobile home in Greenfield behind the home of his co-worker, Don Gerardo Zarco. It wasn't much better than the first trailer, but it provided a safer environment than a labor camp.

Antonio, Meyo and little Teresa enrolled in Greenfield Elementary School. Students in seventh and eighth grades rotated through different classrooms for math, science, English and homeroom. It also had different tracks depending on a student's aptitude. Kili Rendón's parents Tranquilino and *Doña* Amparo rented a house in Greenfield where he also attended Greenfield Elementary. Although young, Antonio was perceptive enough to believe the school system had flaws based on institutional bias.

"Greenfield was the third school I attended in the fall…I was placed in a classroom labeled 'C-Rail' along with other *Mexicanos* and not a single *Americano*. My family decided to remain in Greenfield and the following year my math teacher, Mrs. Campbell, and my English teacher Mrs. Calloway argued my case and the school moved me to the 'A-Rail'.

"This time I was the only *Mexicano* among *Americanos*. The rules of the institution were clear: A-Rail students were tracked into college-bound courses in high school. B-Rail students were tracked into vocational classes. C-Rail students were given a diploma and a work-permit. They were expected to consider themselves lucky for the opportunity to toil in the fields undisturbed by *Migra* (immigration authorities) and to have been taught some English."

Entrance into the A track closed a door on Antonio's past. His friends from Cofradía and many of the boys and girls he knew from farmworker families including Kili[30] were placed in vocational classes. After graduation they transitioned to farms and orchards or moved to vocational schools.

High school and college oriented classes opened new vistas. Antonio's English improved to the point where he no longer made simultaneous translations in his head. He dreamed in his new language. Advance courses in mathematics and science absorbed him. Antonio discovered how chemical formulas and math equations could explain the marvelous workings of the universe and human body.

No matter how much he explained to his father the importance of studies, José only saw Antonio as another pair of hands useful for picking grapes and tomatoes, hoeing rows of lettuce and tying bands around broccoli stalks. Although Antonio excelled in school a university education would be out of the question the moment he could legally work full time.

The summer between Antonio's seventh and eighth grades the Velascos joined hundreds of workers flocking to farms and orchards in "America's Salad Bowl," the Salinas Valley. José's dream of returning to Mexico became a distant longing for a make-believe life in a romantic land of the past.

Teresa had a simpler goal. She was weary of living in temporary labor camps, cramped rented apartments and sleeping in the drafty wreck of a trailer. Teresa wanted a home to call her own.

In the summer of 1966 thirteen-year-old Antonio, eleven-year-old Meyo and eight-year-old Teresa worked with their parents in the carrot fields of Salinas cooled by ocean breezes. By August the valley entered *el invierno Chiquito*, the "short winter" when fields were tilled and fertilized in preparation for planting.

"We heard there was work picking tomatoes in the San Joaquin Valley. My father took us to the small town of Dos Palos near Los Baños about a hundred and forty-five miles south of our home in Greenfield where we lived in Salinas County," Antonio recounted.

Instead of a workers' camp the Velascos and sixty others settled in a stifling barn furnished with cots stacked on top of one another. Water came from taps outside the building. Families tied lines to walls and hung blankets over them to provide a semblance of privacy. Nighttime temperatures inside the barn hovered between ninety and one-hundred-two degrees Fahrenheit.

"We bathed in an irrigation canal because there were no showers. My family walked to the nearby fields. Conditions were deplorable even for me who took every day as an adventure," said Antonio.

David volunteered to repair a tractor on the farm and the owner immediately put him to work as a mechanic and driver paid by the hour and not by the amount of tomatoes everyone else in his family picked. They harvested tomatoes under a harsh, torrid sun. Hour after backbreaking hour they poured tomatoes on conveyor belts that dropped them into large bins hauled away by David sitting high above them in a tractor with an umbrella shielding him from the sun's glare.

Air-conditioned supermarkets throughout the nation stocked cans of whole and diced tomatoes, tomato sauce, and bottles of ketchup. Hundreds of pounds of fresh vegetables Antonio and his family picked came back neatly packaged and labeled. Every vegetable and piece of fruit in supermarkets bore invisible marks of sweat and pain that wracked Antonio's body.

The agony was subservient to the goal of picking tomatoes as fast as possible to bring maximum earnings. His mother worked several rows away from Antonio. She paused and looked across the field at Antonio then stooped to continue working.

After a few minutes Antonio glanced across the rows of tomatoes and saw no sign of Teresa. He stepped over several rows of plants and found his mother writhing on the ground clutching her abdomen and groaning in agony. Tomatoes had spilled from her bucket and splattered under her body.

"I had never seen her like that," recalled Antonio. "My mother was always a very strong woman."

Antonio attempted to help her. She went limp in his arms. He cried for help and José jumped over rows of tomatoes to reach Teresa. Meyo and little Teresa froze when they saw her flailing on the earth. The ranch manager raced into the field in his Jeep. He helped carry Teresa to the Velasco car and directed them to the Dos Palos medical clinic.

Before examining the obviously distressed woman before her, the intake nurse at the clinic shoved forms across the counter and asked for proof of insurance. With no medical coverage, the nurse refused to give permission for admittance. Antonio angrily insisted his sick mother needed immediate attention. It had no impact on the nurse. She ordered them out of the clinic and told them to try the hospital in Los Baños.

The family sped northeast to the emergency entrance of Los Baños Hospital. An intransigent administrator refused to admit the obviously severely ill woman with the excuse she was not a resident of Merced County. The only hospital that would admit her was Natividad [31] in Monterey County at least two hours away.

Teresa's face flushed and she thrashed about calling for her children. She screamed that she needed to collect herbs and struggled to get out of the car. Antonio and José held her down. Teresa's breathing became increasingly labored.

"The emergency room in Dos Palos and the hospital in Los Baños gave her no medication. They didn't even assess or evaluate her condition. It was incredibly painful to see my mother in that situation," Antonio observed. "My father was angry and worried. We all experienced anxiety, depression, sorrow and fear that my mother would die."

By the time they reached Natividad Teresa suffered acute shock. Orderlies rushed her into the emergency room.

70

Nurses and doctors applied intravenous hydration with saline. A doctor advised immediate surgery.

A nurse handed José a form giving the hospital permission to operate. Antonio translated and his father reluctantly signed while murmuring a prayer. David paced back and forth. Meyo and little Teresa held hands. Doctors and nurses scurried in and out of rooms. Hours later a surgeon informed José in Spanish that they removed three benign tumors on her liver. She would have to remain in the hospital for at least one month. In retrospect, Antonio believed his mother's exposure to insecticides and fungicides sprayed on crops may have exacerbated her problem.

Meyo recalled the traumatic event: "In those days they didn't have robotic surgery, so they had to open her up. I remember seeing the long scar stretching across her abdomen and around her side. I cried afraid my mother would not survive.

"For an eleven-year old a month can seem like an eternity during which I had the responsibility of caring for Cecilia and Josefina while my father, David and Antonio worked in the fields. Josefina, only a few months old and two-year old Cecilia sensed that our mother was not there. They would wake in the middle of the night and I had to soothe them back to sleep.

"I also took over my mother's duties. Three-thirty in the morning I got up and made fresh tortillas so that my father and brothers had lunch. My father warned me to stay inside with my sisters. He was afraid that if the police or someone from one of the social agencies visited the camp and found that an eleven-year old was caring for young children without adult supervision we would be taken to a shelter and the county would probably charge my father with neglect. Hiding away didn't work. A visiting nurse came to our trailer and threatened to place all of us in custody."

Their friends the Zarcos jumped into the breach and volunteered to take the children and José into their home while Teresa remained in the hospital. Gerardo Zarco's wife *Doña* Carmen did not work in the fields and could supervise the children. After Antonio went into medical practice the Zarcos became his patients.

José and David took turns driving the children from Greenfield to Salinas and back every evening to visit their mother, a trip of 36 miles in each direction. At the end Teresa was out of danger. The hospital ordered that upon returning home she continue bed rest and medication. Once more the Zarcos came to their rescue and welcomed Teresa into their home where she would be surrounded by family and friends.

The Zarco's old turn-of-the-century home seemed like a palace to Antonio. "It was warm with caring people. The kitchen was large and had a picnic table with benches. We got up in the morning to the aroma of flour tortillas, *chorizo con huevos*, and coffee," Antonio remembered fondly.

"It was near the end of the harvest season sometime in August. Tranquilino Rendón, Jr. and I worked side-by-side during a two-week period when there was less work. The farm gave us five trailers to fill. We began at six in the morning and finished by twelve. Although it was backbreaking work Tranquilino and I made it competitive. The challenge was to fill as many buckets of tomatoes as possible in five hours. Racing each other made us forget the ache and anguish of constantly bending and twisting tomatoes off the plants. By noon I usually filled one hundred twenty buckets. We were paid twenty-five

72

cents for each one. I earned six dollars an hour for five hours work. That was higher than the national minimum wage of one dollar and forty cents an hour. The pace was brutal and could not possibly be maintained for more than five hours at a time."

Antonio sat at Teresa's bedside every evening. His mother who had been the strength and rock of the family seemed unexpectedly vulnerable. She opened her eyes and they held hands. He told Teresa how lucky she was to stay in a comfortable home with Don Gerardo and *Doña* Carmen. Teresa smiled enigmatically and whispered to Antonio that he had a gift and should make the most of it. The transformative moment of his mother's faith and how nurses and doctors performed with care in saving her life placed him on a path from which he never wavered.

Chapter Seven

Wheels

Antonio enviously watched boys and girls in his classes riding bicycles from home to school. He wished he could go with them when they rode to the Salinas River and Arroyo Seco. More than ever he missed the bike David salvaged for him in Somerton.

The window of a local hardware store on El Camino Real near his school featured a red street bicycle on sale for twenty dollars. Antonio ran home and pulled out a box with a portion of wages he saved from the summer harvest. Antonio carefully counted the bills and coins. There was enough money to buy the bike with a little left over.

José believed it was fool-hardy to spend money on what he considered a childish extravaganza. His first reaction was a resounding "no." Antonio calculated a careful response in expectation of his father's rejection. He ticked off reasons why having a bicycle was in the best interest of not only José but the family as well. With his own transportation he could come home sooner to finish his homework. The bicycle would permit him to run errands. In the end, José reluctantly gave permission.

Antonio and his friends wheeled their bikes to Oak Park near the Salinas River where they could see Pinnacles National Monument [32] with its impressive towering domed rock spires.

74

The park had a public swimming pool, swings, and ropes to climb. Antonio played impromptu soccer and basketball with Kili and other friends. During those rare tranquil moments Antonio lived the ideal American life. He played with ferocious focus and always to win.

"He liked sports but would rather spend his time reading and studying. He wanted us to do the same. Antonio convinced a few friends but most of us wanted to play basketball and soccer. I think it's because he enjoyed the competition," Kili reminisced.

Immersing himself in studies helped Antonio overcome the emotional trauma of his mother's surgery. David gave up his job in Dos Palos one hundred forty miles away to be near Teresa. With his work as a tractor driver plus his mechanical aptitude he obtained a permanent position in Greenfield as trucking manager for Basic Vegetable Products a union organized processing company that produced and packaged spices.

José abandoned the migrant farmworker trail to remain close to Teresa. Serendipitously, Basic Vegetables hired him as a forklift driver with guaranteed wages and health and pension benefits. After Teresa recovered and returned home, David and José arranged with the plant manager to hire her for a less taxing job in the packing department. For the first time since leaving Mexico the Velascos had permanence in their lives. The children would not have to change schools according to harvest schedules.

Antonio entered the eighth grade "A" track in Greenfield Elementary. He and one other student were the only Hispanics in the class. At first he felt estranged although he never recalled signs of racial tension. Students on the same track respected one another.

During recess and lunch he gravitated to Hispanic school friends. Several had emigrated with their families from San Luis Rio Colorado to Greenfield. His best friends were Juan and Lupe Zarco sons of the family that took them in while Teresa Velasco recovered from surgery.

Antonio recalled Juan and Kili's support and encouragement even though they were relegated to the vocational track. After eighth grade their paths would diverge. Many students in the vocational track dropped out of school and returned to work in the fields with their families.

Antonio graduated in the top percentile of Greenfield Elementary in 1967 and planned to enroll in King City High School when his father decided that with Basic Vegetables closing down for the Christmas holiday the family would return to Mexico for a protracted stay.

Once again José delayed returning to California while he threw parties for family and friends. Meyo complained she would be left behind in school. Antonio adamantly complained that his first year in high school would be disastrous if he missed the first week.

Teresa angrily ordered Jose to pack up and leave for Greenfield. He needed to consider his children before his own pleasure. Their jobs at Basic might not wait until they returned. Teresa then dropped the news she was pregnant and needed to return home before it became difficult to travel.

High school presented challenges to Antonio's self-esteem. Although his grades qualified him for the "A" track he had doubts he could maintain them. "I worked hard to make up the deficiency caused by my father's initial intransigence. In a short time I caught up. My teachers recommended me to the California Scholarship Federation (CSF).[33] Membership in CSF was demanding. I needed to follow specific course lists that included intellectually and academically challenging material, extensive amounts of reading and writing in English and Spanish, critical thinking and problem solving, and individual science lab work."

Adhering to the California Scholarship Foundation curriculum gave students credits for entry into the University of California as long as they maintained a high-grade point average. Antonio's academic achievements did not allay his anxiety.

"I felt afraid of the unknown. I had no friends in high school. I had no idea what to expect from boys who were four years older and much bigger. I thought they might bully me. I didn't know if I could defend myself."

In the mid-twentieth century endemic bigotry ran deep in Greenfield and King City. Social and economic polarization endured between Anglo Americans and Mexican farm laborers. Fortunately the rarified group of college-bound students accepted Antonio's scholastic competency and recognized his academic intellect.

"Initially I felt discomfort in my new surroundings. However no one in any of my classes ever demonstrated prejudice toward me," Antonio reminisced. He became friends with studious and intellectually curious students from a variety of backgrounds.

"By default we hung out together. I knew my English wasn't perfect," he recalled. "The school was large, and I had classes in different rooms divided among several buildings. Student populations in classrooms were not homogeneous."

"A" track students had their eyes set on college and competed with ferocity for high grades knowing that those who fell below a B average would be relegated to a "B" or "C" track.

"It was daunting. I felt as if I had fallen behind and it often embarrassed me. I remember that in the eighth grade just before graduation I wrote an essay about the Industrial Revolution and Cyrus McCormick the inventor of the mechanical reaping machine. I had to read it aloud to the class. In my essay I referred to the invention as a 'raping' machine. The whole class erupted in laughter. I sat there not knowing what I said. No one, not even the teacher explained my error to me."

Another major challenge faced him, one that echoed his brother's trauma that abruptly changed his life moving from an academic life to farm worker after performing successfully at the Commercial Industrial Technical Institute in San Luis Rio Colorado. Antonio feared that when he reached his sixteenth or seventeenth birthday his father would demand he drop out of school. It would crush his hopes just as it crushed David's future.

"My father wanted me to work at Basic when I graduated high school," Antonio recollected. "It was a good job for my parents. David worked in the plant and my father spoke with the factory manager about me. But I wanted to continue my education."

A few months later his mother returned to Natividad Hospital in Salinas and gave birth to a girl, Dolores. José Velasco saw his daughters as a major encumbrance that could only be solved if Antonio joined David working at Basic Vegetables.

Antonio considered a variety of plans to overcome his father's determination that he enters the labor force. He devised an agenda to graduate from high school in three years and attend college prior to his eighteenth birthday.

"Everyone in high school took seven classes. It was routine that one of the classes could be Study Hall that had no credits. Not me. I decided to take seven solids that would give me three additional classes the equivalent of a whole year," recounted Antonio.

King City High School offered a work-study program designed for students on a vocational track that granted class credit for work. Antonio took advantage of it to accelerate his path through high school.

He approached Ted the manager of King City High School maintenance and asked for a job after school as part of his work-study program. Asked why an "A" track student would use a vocational program, Antonio explained that additional credits would help him graduate in three years. He could apply to college early and get a head start toward his college degree.

"Ted hired me as his chief assistant. Most of the work was completed in two hours and the other maintenance men would drink coffee or talk until their shift finished. I also took over the chore of cleaning the school library," said Antonio. "Time permitting, Ted told me to find a book or do my homework."

After a few weeks observing Antonio's diligence and willingness to take on additional maintenance tasks, Ted suggested Antonio meet Roy Garlinger who owned and operated two gas stations in King City, one across the street from high school and another on the north end of town.

Hours and working conditions were better. Antonio could earn money and continue to receive class credit. Years later Antonio discovered Ted's motivation for helping him. The maintenance man could neither read nor write. He saw what he could have been in the teenager.

Garlinger, a big, rugged, plainspoken individual hired Antonio to open the station in the early morning before school started. When Garlinger's full-time employees showed up Antonio crossed the street to attend classes. He returned in the afternoon to close shop. In the era prior to self-service stations Antonio pumped fuel for autos, washed car windows, changed and repaired tires, and learned to take care of minor tune-ups.

Antonio spent time outdoors dealing with customers who appreciated his dedication and affability that often resulted in repeat business. When he had no customers Garlinger insisted Antonio concentrate on his schoolwork.

At the end of each week Garlinger reconciled receipts from gas pumps and auto repairs. Over time discrepancies he couldn't reconcile showed up in his books. Antonio noticed the station owner's frustration. Off-handedly Garlinger mentioned the problem to the young boy.

Antonio asked permission to examine the books. Amused by the teen's curiosity Garlinger permitted him to look over his shoulder. Within a few minutes Antonio detected a divergence between fuel sales and auto repair sales. The boy's deductive reasoning impressed the station owner who temporarily turned over the task of balancing receipts to the teenager.

Antonio compiled a worksheet that pointed to the possible problem. Credit cards did not become popular until

1973 and service stations were cash businesses. Gas pumps registered gallons of gas sold therefore income from fuel sales was easy to control. The teenager uncovered variances in the ledger that could only occur if one or more of Garlinger's employees skimmed off auto repair fees.

Garlinger undertook a daily tally of auto repair transactions. He confirmed that an employee siphoned a few dollars from repair jobs. Garlinger immediately fired the mechanic and placed Antonio in charge of all his bookkeeping.

A few months later he bought another gas station close to the newly built Interstate 101 Freeway. Although the three service stations had slightly different accounting systems Antonio mastered them and eventually proved indispensable. As business grew Garlinger hired a lead auto mechanic from the local community. Lloyd arrived in the morning after Antonio opened the station. The mechanic remained until school ended and Antonio returned.

High school also opened new perspectives for Antonio. The 'A' track brought together students from diverse backgrounds: transplanted mid-westerners, children of families who escaped the Dust Bowl[34] of the 1930s, Latinos and Asians.

In the late nineteenth century the Salinas Valley experienced a large influx of immigrants escaping massacres committed by the Ottoman Empire against the small independent nation of Armenia. They settled in the fertile valley where they gave impetus to the raisin industry that became the foundation for the area economy.

In his high school sophomore year Antonio met Clayton Abajian[35] from an Armenian-American family. Clayton's mother coordinated English as a Second Language programs for children of migrant farm workers. His father retired from the U.S. Air Force and opened an auto repair shop opposite Garlinger's service station.

While Antonio delved into chemistry and physiology, Clayton had an affinity for technology and radio broadcasting. The operator of a 1000-watt radio station in King City offered the clever sixteen-year old a job as program manager and disk jockey.

Clayton often dropped in to visit Antonio after his father closed his repair shop. "Pumping gas and working on cars seemed more fun than broadcasting," he recalled. "I gave up my job at the radio station to work for Roy [Garlinger] with Tony. We both loved cars, and this gave me an opportunity to learn more about retail sales."

Impressed by Antonio's pro-social consciousness as well as intellectual prowess Clayton's mother fostered the relationship between the boys. His mother giggled and whispered, that Antonio reminded her of the actor Ricardo Montalbán because he was 'cool' and very special.

"She let me hang out with him in the hope that Tony would rub off on me," Clayton said.

Antonio's Civics instructor recognized the innate sense of social justice Clayton's mother observed. He arranged the class as a mock House of Representatives. Antonio won an overwhelming election as leader of the house.

"I developed my verbal skills and more and more awareness of what I could accomplish," Antonio said reflecting back to that time.

The summer after his sophomore semester he enrolled in Hartnell Junior College, Salinas, California for courses necessary to graduate at the end of the eleventh grade.

"College is a waste of time, " José complained.

His mother reinforced and encouraged her son's goal. Looking back at the split between his parents Antonio suspected his mother carried an enormous amount of guilt by not supporting his brother David when José demanded he work as a farm hand.

Antonio's sister Meyo remembered her mother standing up to José about Antonio's goal. "Don't worry about your father," their mother said. "He'll come around."

Meyo recalled her father grousing: "He's going to grow up and be a hippy. Tony's not going because there's drugs and alcohol in college. The people are lazy, and they'll spoil him."

Teresa insisted that Antonio was a hard worker and would earn far more money as a college graduate. There was no way to satisfy her husband. According to Meyo he dragged one of Antonio's friends into the argument.

"Tranquilino's driving a tractor. He makes more money than I made working two jobs."

"Do what you need to do," Teresa advised Antonio. "You're working twenty hours a day between school and jobs to earn your way to college."

Teresa won the argument. Antonio mastered the core curriculum for the California Federation of Scholarships, continued his work-study program, and attended summer school.

Clayton Abajian assumed that he and Antonio would graduate from high school together. "I felt disappointed [that he would graduate one year earlier] but Tony was definitely in the minority of high achievers at King City High School. My mother talked to him about going to college." It didn't diminish their relationship. Antonio was Best Man at Clayton's wedding in 1973.

Students beginning their junior semester in high school had to keep up their Grade Point Average (GPA) and take the Scholastic Assessment Test (SAT) to qualify for entry into University of California schools. Richard Meyer, son of the King City mayor Emil C. Meyer, was a year older than Antonio and had a driver's license. He also intended to graduate in three years. Together they drove to San Luis Obispo for their SATs.

Before returning home they traveled north to the University of California, Santa Cruz. Set amid a bucolic redwood forest on the slopes of the Santa Cruz Mountains, the school had a pastoral atmosphere. Footbridges spanned creeks rushing through ravines. The Great Meadow, an untouched nature preserve where bobcats roamed made up the southern border of the university. Golden Eagles and Red-tailed Hawks soared overhead. Antonio immediately knew the campus would be his destination no matter how much his father objected.

Elva García, the young girl who attended fifth grade with Antonio in Somerton, Arizona arrived in Greenfield with her mother, father, sisters and brothers and enrolled as a freshman at King City High School in 1969. To her surprise she met Antonio on campus. Although they were the same age, Antonio had entered his third year due to his Somerton teacher Mrs. Plotts recommendation to skip a full year.

"I admired Antonio's intelligence, dedication, and determination. He was completely focused on school always reading and doing homework. When he graduated in three years I was very proud of him. I had no idea how he did it," reported Elva.

After high school graduation the Greenfield School District employed Elva. She worked alongside Antonio's sisters Meyo and Teresa. It resulted in a strong relationship with Antonio's mother. It was a fortunate circumstance. Elva met Antonio's friend Tranquilino (Kili) Rendón, Jr. who had left farm work to become an electrician.

Elva studied real estate and accounting at Hartnell College. Eventually she worked at Sacramento City College in administration. In 1975 she married Kili Rendón. Ten years later Antonio became her obstetrician and delivered her youngest daughter Vanessa.

"My second child was born at home with the aid of midwife. When Antonio heard about it he said 'No, no, no. You need a doctor.' With my third child he insisted I go to the hospital where he delivered my girl with no complications."

In January 1969, long before he achieved his dream of becoming a doctor, Antonio achieved another goal: he qualified for a driver's permit. David taught him to drive in his white Lincoln Continental convertible.

"We would drive up Highway 101 to Salinas with the top down," Antonio recalled nostalgically. "David took his hands off the steering wheel and told me to take over. It wasn't the safest thing to do, but someone had to steer the car. Later he permitted me to sit in the driver's seat."

Antonio fantasized about having his own car. It seemed impossible until a tow truck pulled a battered 1956 two-door Chevrolet Bel-Air with a burned-out engine to the service station. The owner never showed up to take possession and the car sat at the station for months.

The State of California required abandoned automobiles be placed on sale for thirty days and sold to the highest bidder. Upon the sale of the car the Department of Motor Vehicles received half the revenue. Garlinger obeyed the letter of the law. He placed a "for sale" sign on the car door window. In the morning he opened the car door so that the sign faced inward where no one could see it. After thirty days Garlinger gave the car to Antonio as a gift for his sixteenth birthday.

Garlinger's mechanic Lloyd worked tirelessly after hours rebuilding the engine from the ground up. When finished, he presented it to the high school teenager. Antonio had no way to pay Lloyd. The mechanic said it was his way of helping him get to college.

Although the car ran as if new, paint flaked off its body. Stuffing and springs popped out the upholstery. Antonio and Clayton asked their mothers for permission to drive to San Luis Rio Colorado, Mexico where the car could be painted and reupholstered at a fraction of the cost than in the States. The Velascos permitted Antonio to go as long as Clayton drove with him. His parents saw Antonio as highly responsible and had no qualms about the two of them driving across the border.

The boys took the reverse route driven by the Velascos when they made their way to California and the Salinas Valley from Somerton, Arizona. The road stretched through sun-scorched Imperial Valley and along the shores of the briny inland Salton Sea, a vast three-hundred forty-three square mile depression created by an ancient earthquake. A breach in a Colorado River canal resulted in a massive two-year flood filling the basin. With no exit it became saltier than the Pacific Ocean. Desert, mesas, and gray, pink, and red sandstone dominated

86

the landscape. Relics of fish traps built by Native-Americans tracked up the slopes providing evidence that a sea rose and fell in the area over many cycles through the centuries.

"The car stalled north of a small town called Westmoreland," Clayton remembered. "The Salton Sea was less than a mile away. We took a nap in the shade of the front bumper until the car cooled down. When we got up we used our modest mechanic skills and the car started. We drove to Westmoreland, rented a room at a motel and waited for a mechanic the next morning. He didn't find anything wrong with the car."

They drove through Somerton, Arizona, the same town where Antonio's remedial teacher recommended placement in a mainstream classroom, the first step in his long, arduous climb up the education ladder.

"The car stalled again about three miles past Somerton and five miles from San Luis," said Clayton. "I called my uncle who had worked with my father in the auto repair business and described the situation. He diagnosed it and drove all the way down to the border with a new part. We continued our journey to San Luis. For me the adventure was being in a foreign country and barely speaking or understanding the language. Tony was my savior and he pretty much kept me out of trouble."

Chapter Eight

The Battle to Succeed

By the end of his first semester as a junior Antonio amassed almost four years' worth of credits. At the close of the school year he planned to apply at U.C. Santa Cruz. An unforeseen obstacle cut short his ambitious goal. The school required that all students have the equivalent of four years physical education in order to graduate. Undaunted he took two P. E. classes in his junior year.

Meyo entered ninth grade at King City High School and on several occasions Antonio drove her to school in his rebuilt Chevrolet. "I thought I was riding in a chariot. Going to phys. ed. twice a day for a whole semester turned my brother into a muscular, well-built guy. When girls saw my brother with his own car they wanted to meet him."

Antonio was oblivious to the attention of girls until the six-foot tall daughter of one of the area's largest farm owners begged Meyo to ask him to take her to the senior prom. After multiple entreaties from his sister, five-foot seven-inch Antonio reluctantly acquiesced. It was not the date he envisioned on his first prom.

It was a daring move for Antonio who continued to live with the same fear of the unknown he experienced the day he left his small village of Cofradía de Suchitlán in the Mexican Highlands. Every step he took upward was fraught with anxiety. The dream in which he saw himself in a movie played over and over in his sleep.

Mystery and danger lurked beyond the veil of clouds descending over the volcano where lava flowed carrying death and nutrition into the valleys. Antonio did not know from one day to the next if he would face insurmountable obstacles or nourishment from his desire to learn and move out of the life into which his brother was forced.

An existential crisis emerged as the date of Antonio's graduation approached. He never forgot the heroic doctors at Natividad Hospital who brought his mother back from the brink of death. He fantasized about becoming a healer, a physician who could make a difference in the lives of men, women and children. The aspiration seemed unattainable. The cycle of farm work, moving from harvest to harvest, felt ingrained in his psyche. Antonio was unaware that two years prior to high school graduation in 1971 events in the nation's capital took place that would eventually have a major impact on his future.

The Senate Subcommittee on Migratory Labor chaired by Senator Walter F. Mondale[36] of Minnesota held hearings concerning the difficulty farmworkers faced working in fields sprayed with toxic pesticides.

James D. Lorenz, Associate Director of California Rural Legal Assistance from Los Angeles provided detailed testimony of poisoning incidents. "Twice in the last two weeks, a number of farmworkers have been sprayed by crop dusters while they were working in the fields of a strawberry grower. Their employer does not make a practice of telling his workers what he sprays his field with, nor does he take various safety precautions to ensure that they will not be subjected to such accidents, as he is required to do so by various provisions of the California Labor Code. Moreover, when informed of such accidents, the State Department of Agriculture and the local Agricultural Commissioner have refused to release information as to what pesticides and fertilizers the grower has been using, even though such refusals violated the California's Freedom of Information Act. Not knowing what they have been sprayed with, the farmworkers are unable to secure proper medication from local doctors; for, as several leading medical experts have recently testified, doctors cannot provide adequate treatment for pesticide injury when they do not know what the ailing worker was sprayed with.

"The result? An average of two farmworkers die each year from pesticide poisoning in California and the agricultural industry in California has an occupational disease rate which is fifty percent higher than that of the next highest industry and almost three times as high as the average disease rate of all industries.

"A significant number of these fatalities and injuries have occurred, medical experts say, because of the lack of safety precautions by employers (even those precautions required by law) and because of the general lack of information about insecticides (even though the State Department of Agriculture is required to release such information). Violations of the law can be costly."[37]

Senator Mondale held additional hearings in September 1971. Anthony Bianco, Jr. president of Bianco Fruit Corporation one of the largest grape growers in the United States headquartered in Fresno, California came under intense questioning regarding harmful pesticides.

Mr. Bianco testified: "I am the grower of the Thompson seedless grapes which were presented to this subcommittee on August 1st as containing harmful levels of the pesticide Aldrin.[38] Specifically, the report on my grapes by the C. W. England Laboratories said the Aldrin content was 18 parts per million...or 180 times the established human tolerance level. The England report says UFWOC [United Farmworkers of California] advised the laboratory the grapes in question came from my operation in the Coachella Valley. I did not ship any Thompson seedless grapes from the Coachella Valley to Washington."

Sen. Mondale asked Mr. Bianco: "Are you seeking to establish that the grapes which the farmworkers, and later Safeway, submitted to England Laboratories... were not grapes from your farm?"

Mr. Bianco responded: "No...But these grapes weren't in the same condition as when they left my vineyards.... No grower in the Coachella Valley or Kern County—and that includes Delano and Arvin—uses Aldrin on grapes. I don't know of any grape grower anywhere who uses Aldrin on grapes... The Food and Drug Administration [FDA] survey on its sixty tests in market and packer samplings across the country found no trace of Aldrin on any grapes, including mine, which were specifically tested by the FDA. I resent the tactic that has been used against me. This Aldrin scare is no more than another effort to whip me into submission."

"Would you say Safeway also uses Aldrin as part of that effort to whip you into submission?" queried Sen. Mondale.

"No, " responded Mr. Bianco. "I tried to negotiate [with the United Farmworkers of California] but could get nowhere in the face of UFWOC's nonnegotiable demands. Now UFWOC is trying to bring me down in retaliation. What has happened here is contrary to the stated principles of César Chávez and his movement… He failed to persuade workers on farms to join his organization. He staged a boycott aimed at forcing union organization by pressuring stores. Now he has moved to this new tactic of trying to destroy an industry with the false charge of pesticide contamination."

"When Mr. Chávez testified, I think he indicated that he had wired the growers indicating that he was willing to yield some on the wage issue if you were willing to accept more effective controls, as the wine grape growers have, in contracts on pesticides," stated Sen. Mondale.

Mr. Bianco fired back: "The California Rural Legal Assistance [CRLA], an organization financed with Federal funds and whose board of directors includes César Chávez, has filed several nuisance suits against grape growers. One was filed against me, which my attorneys say is only further harassment. This UFWOC pesticide campaign is false."

Sen. Mondale pressed Mr. Bianco. "Are you satisfied that in the fields of Southern California where the grape workers toil, that they are fully protected from any pesticide poisoning which might affect their health or their life? … Then how do you feel about the survey…which said that of the workers surveyed, eighty percent had symptoms of pesticide injuries? Or the work of Dr. Irma West,[39] who is with the State of California, which said that occupational disease in agriculture is a number one problem and three times higher than the average of all industries, and that 3,000 children are treated for ingestion of pesticides every year? In addition to that, of course, HEW [Health, Education and Welfare] and

92

they included California in their survey estimates, testified that perhaps as many as 800 people die a year from pesticides, and that possibly as many as 80,000 are injured. Do you think it is fair to say then that this exposure to the pesticides problem raised by the farmworkers is a scare tactic? Are you willing to testify that it is a trumped-up charge, and that the farmworker's health is not risked by pesticides? ... Now suppose you were just a neutral citizen, living in Washington, D.C. You liked grapes, and you were not interested in this boycott at all. But, in the health of your children, and you were wealthy enough to decide that you wanted to test grapes for pesticide residues. What reasonable step would you take to test the grapes?"

"To do what? I didn't get that," answered Mr. Bianco.

"You just wanted to find out if grapes in Washington, D.C, have pesticides on them to determine whether you want your family to eat them. What would you do? What would be a fair thing to do?" asked Sen. Mondale.

"I would wash the grapes and eat them. I have a lot of faith in our Government agencies that if there was anything wrong with the products, I am sure it would not be for sale," Mr. Bianco responded.

Sen. Mondale pursued the subject. "Suppose you went down to the Safeway and you bought a bunch of grapes and you took it to England Laboratories, and England Laboratories came up and said they had 18 p.p.m. residue of Aldrin, and you were disturbed, so you wrote a letter to the editor setting forth what the test showed. Do you think that would be false and irresponsible on the part of the citizen?"

"...Why would I take a bunch of grapes from a store to a laboratory?" responded Mr. Bianco.

"Suppose you were the president of Safeway, and you were concerned, and you decided you wanted to know whether there was Aldrin on those grapes or not. So you took three tests...[because] your major concern as a store president, is protection of your customers, which is very important. You have routinely over the years used these same laboratories to determine whether or not the consumers are protected, and you took those tests, and three out of four came back with findings of Aldrin, and you were concerned. Would you think that was irresponsible on the part of Safeway? What did the farmworkers do that was different in their test?" queried Sen. Mondale.

Mr. Bianco responded, "Why did they take the grapes to the laboratory?"

Incredulous, Sen. Mondale replied: "I am not asking you to be a psychiatrist, I am asking you what did they do that was different? Do you think that your statement in your handout yesterday that this is a false pesticide scare is a fair characterization of what they did?"

Mr. Bianco answered: "We were warned about this."

"Do you think it was irresponsible on their part to take grapes and have them tested at an independent laboratory saying that was the same that Safeway uses? Is it possible that what exists here is an honest difference of opinion, and not a false and irresponsible effort?"

Mr. Bianco replied, "It is possible."[40]

In a hearing the previous year on April 15, 1970 the Deputy Director of California Rural Legal Assistance Robert Gnaizda testified. "Three decades ago, John Steinbeck recorded the Joad family's futile struggle to earn fifteen cents an hour

94

while competing with 300,000 surplus farmworkers brought to California by grower promises that outweighed the available jobs in order to depress wages and working conditions...

"Despite the 1933 Wagner-Peyser Act,[41] and despite some glorious rhetoric, the only significant change for the migratory farmworker since the Thirties is that the grower has been joined by one of the most powerful and wealthy, albeit benign corporations in America, the federally-supported and sponsored State Farm Labor Service...

"A former California Farm Labor Office employee, and ex-mayor of Hollister, recently filed an affidavit with a Federal Court in San Francisco that conditions for the farmworker had not materially changed since the 1930's...

"...Despite the harm to 37,500 California farmworkers caused by excessive use of dangerous pesticides by employers, no farm labor office requires growers to even provide a list of pesticides being used. The Farm Labor Office has not provided any counseling or any testing to any farmworkers, despite federal regulations requiring such counseling...

"...On February 20, 1970, thirty farm workers met with Secretary of Labor [George] Shultz in San Francisco, asked him to obey his own rules and regulations, and presented to him a Farm Worker Bill of Rights that could help end the unseemly government sponsorship and support of 'Grapes of Wrath' and 'Harvest of Shame' conditions.... rights promised by the Wagner-Peyser Act."[42]

Hearings on dangers to farmworkers did little to prevent abuses. Rampant improper practices continued throughout the state and nation due to the enormous influence of money spent on a lobbying consortium of corporate farms, chemical companies, and pesticide applicators.

The *San Francisco Chronicle* reported blowback by chemical companies against critics of pesticides. Dow Chemicals fought strenuously against an emergency standard issued by the Environmental Protection Agency in August 1977 that limited airborne exposure to dibromochloropropane (DBCP,) a chemical linked to sterility in chemical plant workers.

"Dr. Paul Gehring, Dow's chief toxicologist, spent two hours at the hearing on an exhaustive summary of scientific tests of DBCP, and concluded that extremely stiff emergency standards effectively banning its manufacture are unnecessary... His defense of manufacture of the substance... came despite the discovery of at least 95 pesticide workers nationwide who are infertile or sterile following prolonged exposure to DBCP."[43]

Chapter Nine

Specter of Bigotry

Unaware of political and corporate maneuvering to maintain agribusiness and chemical company status quo Antonio focused on completing high school and entering university.

Antonio Velasco King City High School graduation, 1970. (Velasco Family Archive)

"On one hand I had become more self-assured. On the other I had the underlying fear that I was a fraud and couldn't compete," recalled Antonio.

Impressed with his bilingual facility and math and science scholarship his Spanish teacher Mrs. Averhoff called him to her office for what he thought would be a reprimand for an unknown error in his work. He sat down nervously waiting to hear the worst. Mrs. Averhoff shuffled through a few papers he recognized as his homework assignments.

"Tony, I've been discussing you with your other teachers. We all believe you have a remarkable aptitude for science. I think you should go to medical school in Spain," she counseled.

The inconceivable notion that he would travel six thousand miles to Spain to study medicine seemed ludicrous. He asked her why she thought Spain was a good idea. She responded that American medical schools could be problematic for a Spanish-speaking immigrant from a farming family. Spain would view Antonio as an American who had the asset of speaking fluent Spanish. Antonio respected his teacher's assessment and her conviction in his abilities. Internally he had difficulty reconciling Mrs. Averhoff's confidence and his self-image.

Meyo had no doubts about his teacher's suggestion. "I told him he was good in math and science and could become a doctor. In our culture that was the highest calling you could have."

As weeks dragged by waiting for his SAT scores the idea presented by Mrs. Averhoff and his sister's faith in his abilities percolated within. A few weeks later Antonio received a letter listing his high scores. He had jumped a major hurdle and immediately filled out an application to enroll at the University of California Santa Cruz. With his SATs and transcripts attached he presented it for his counselor's signature. The counselor looked askance at the short, dark-skinned Mexican boy with a heavy accent.

"You have to be smart and have good grades to go to UCSC," Antonio recalled him saying without looking at documents that demonstrated his scholastic achievements.

The counselor's insensitive, bigoted reaction brought back the specter of his placement in a class for mentally challenged children when he entered elementary school in Somerton, Arizona. The days of not being assertive and withdrawing into a cocoon vanished. Antonio forcefully demanded his counselor send the application to the university.

He shoved Antonio's paperwork in an envelope. "Are you satisfied, Mr. Velasco?" he snapped.

Vindicated, Antonio waited anxiously for his invitation to enroll. A classmate who was a King City High School Senior received notification that Santa Cruz had accepted him although he had a lower GPA and SAT than Antonio. A few days later he experienced shock and disappointment when he received a letter of rejection.

He sped north to the university campus where he met with the administrator of the Education Opportunity Program[44] Roberto Rubalcava. He informed Antonio he was rejected because he was only a junior in high school. The paperwork sent to the university failed to include the required SAT scores and transcripts demonstrating he satisfactorily met all requirements for high school graduation and enrollment at Santa Cruz.

Antonio confronted his high school counselor who suggested sarcastically Antonio had to take special remedial classes to qualify. The casual, insensitive remark revealed deep-rooted prejudice against the children of migrant farm workers.

Indignantly Antonio dropped his transcripts and SAT scores on the counselor's desk. "Read these and tell me I'm not qualified," he insisted. "I'll wait right here and make sure you sign it off. If you refuse I will report you to the school administrator for dereliction of duty."

Faced with his indefensible posture the counselor reluctantly certified that Antonio completed all coursework necessary to graduate high school at the end of his junior year and could apply for admission to UCSC.

"I immediately drove back to the Santa Cruz campus where Roberto Rubalcava gave his stamp of approval," said Antonio.

The university environment had changed since his last visit. Turmoil, anger and protests over the Vietnam War, racism, and dysfunction in government were rampant. It came to a head on May 4, 1970 when Ohio National Guard troops quelled an anti-war demonstration on the campus of Kent State University in Kent, Ohio. They indiscriminately fired into the crowd of demonstrators killing four students and wounding nine others.

Unrest erupted throughout the country at universities, colleges and high schools. Dire reports from Vietnam instigated a national dialogue about the efficacy of the United States' role in a civil war on the Asian peninsula and the illegal unexpected invasion of Cambodia ordered by President Richard Nixon.

100

Campus turbulence worried Antonio's mother. Every day the news reported dissension. Television images of rebellious students compounded her anxiety. Rumors spread that protests were the product of Communists, drunks, and drug addicts.

Teresa knew that Antonio and his sisters had *una buena cabeza y un buen corazón*, a good head and good heart. She steeled herself against the constant pummeling from the media with stories of unrest and resolved to make sure he had the opportunity denied to his brother David.

Meyo recalled the day Antonio announced his desire to go to the university. Her father "made no bones that he thought Antonio going off to college was like treachery to him. Dad was left alone with the immense burden of supporting five girls. At best we would marry well but it would do him no good. Worst case scenario: we would become pregnant and bring additional mouths home for him to feed and clothe."[45]

In José's own words "If Tony went to work with me he would soon become a *gorra cuadrada*, a square hardhat—a foreman at the spice factory."

His friends were overwhelmed that Santa Cruz had accepted him. Kili Rendón drove a tractor, had a new car, and made a good living. He asked how long Antonio would have to stay in school.

"Eight or ten years? That's ridiculous. How can you stay in school that long? Suppose you spend all those years studying and don't make it? You're thinking about a career that's going to take a long time. You could make a good living right now," Kili insisted.

Kili and friends with whom he had grown up viewed their future as an extension of current circumstances and little could change. Moving to a new stage in life didn't compute as long as they met their immediate needs: food on the table, clothing, a home, and a car. Years later those same *compadres* came to him as patients. He saw them through illnesses, pregnancies, ministered to their needs.

Antonio carried in his memory the agony of debilitating physical work where every muscle in his body screamed with pain; where thorns on lemon trees pierced his fingers and hands; his back froze, and he could barely stand. Sitting inflicted shocks and aching nerves to his entire system.

The University of California, Santa Cruz admitted Antonio in 1971 one month after his eighteenth birthday breaking the chain tying him to the circle of life that destroyed his brother's future.

The city of Santa Cruz evoked scenes from idealistic college themed motion pictures. Victorian homes stood on almost every corner. Early twentieth-century brick buildings housing coffee shops, art galleries, and new and used bookstores where U.C. students gathered lined Pacific Avenue. A 1911 carousel on Beach Boardwalk sent festive calliope music into the air. Children rocked up and down on old ornate hand-carved horses. Joyous screams echoed over the beach from riders on the Big Dipper wood rollercoaster built in 1924.

He drove beyond Santa Cruz Wharf up High Street through the entrance to the campus passing the Barn Theatre, a weatherworn ranch building dating back to the nineteenth century. Antonio wended his way up Coolidge Drive into an evocative landscape of ancient Redwood trees, lush undergrowth and giant ferns reminding him of Cofradía.

Six years elapsed since he crossed the border into the United States on an unimaginable journey of possibilities. In this new environment Antonio pushed into a dark corner the entanglement of life lived on the edge of poverty.

He spent his first days in the confusing milieu of dormitory assignment, course counseling, and class registration. Pre-medical courses had no undergraduate degrees available and medical schools did not require a specific major as long as students met core requirements. Antonio's science and math skills gave him multiple options. "After researching various majors I decided on chemistry. It didn't appear competitive and could lead to a career," Antonio said in retrospect.

The university assigned him to Crown College a residence housing chemistry majors and pre-medical students. One of the advantages Santa Cruz offered was a revolutionary grading system. For most of its academic life, the university favored a 'Pass/Fail' system. Instead of grades professors wrote student evaluations.

Education Opportunity Program students arrived on campus prior to the start of the freshman school year. The multitude of bright and talented students came from families with similar backgrounds as Antonio. Kili's dismay that he might stay in college for years and fail haunted Antonio's outlook. He was determined to overcome his personal demons.

"I needed to join others from my socio-economic background who could help me navigate life outside of my self-built boundaries. That's when I found MEChA[46] (*Moviemento Estudiantil Chicano de Aztlán*-Chicano Student Movement of Aztlán) a radical Hispanic movement, led by Roberto Rubalcava who helped me enter Santa Cruz," Antonio reminisced.

A political activist in California's Central Valley where the majority of Chicano farm workers labored, Rubalcava's charismatic personality attracted radical affluent Latino students born primarily in the United States. MEChA's demographic makeup did not mesh with immigrant Mexicans who laboriously succeeded in attaining what their families imagined as entering the rarified atmosphere of higher education. Antonio hoped the organization would exceed his expectations and decided to remain with the Chicano student society where he met pre-med sophomore Jeff Solinas. [47]

Jeff's parents George and Rita Solinas were militants in the Chicano movement. Rita received her Master's degree in psychology from the University of California, Santa Barbara. George worked for Self Help International [48] in Washington, D.C. an organization dedicated to alleviating world hunger and poverty.

George met Manuel Chávez at Self Help. He introduced him to his brother César Chávez the founder of the United Farm Workers (UFW). Chávez, a high school dropout from Yuma, Arizona worked as a migrant farm worker before serving two years in the United States Navy. Chávez and Dolores Huerta, a leader with a magnetic personality, whose father Juan Fernandez had been a union activist and California State Assemblyman, co-founded the National Farm Workers Association that eventually became the United Farm Workers.

Chávez asked George Solinas to join the UFW and assist in building Agbayani Village a retirement community in Delano, California for retired Philippine farm workers. George concentrated on the retirement village. Rita became a psychological counselor for the union.

The UFW and MEChA fought against established norms from different perspectives. The UFW concentrated on action, wages, and worker rights. MEChA successfully placed

104

political pressure on educational institutions to incorporate Chicano studies in their curricula.

The organization met resistance from non-Hispanics who believed a conspiracy theory it intended to revolt against the state and elect a Latino political senate and legislature in California as prelude to forming the new state of Aztlán the name of the mythical Aztec ancestral home.

Antonio experienced visceral excitement in the dynamics of the movement. MEChA gave him additional self-assurance although he soon discovered that its hardcore leaders viewed established institutions as the enemy. As time progressed discrimination within the organization emerged.

"In a strange way they were prejudiced against Hispanics who came from farmworker backgrounds and who had pronounced accents. They did their best to treat me as a second-class citizen," expressed Antonio.

The image he initially had about the pastoral, cinematic version of the university as a poster child for fantasy college musicals ended rapidly. Raucous rallies against the Vietnam War took place weekly. Usually peaceful, on occasion demonstrators would occupy administration offices in concert with UC Berkeley and UC Davis.

Four-hundred fifty-thousand young men and women of color mostly from lower and middle class backgrounds fought in the front lines of the Vietnam War.[49] They hoped service in the armed forces would provide opportunity to eventually receive veteran benefits. The majority of college students across the United States avoided the draft.

Antonio undertook a serious examination of MEChA's attitude toward those in his socioeconomic strata. Disadvantaged students of color needed more than slogans. They needed financial and psychological support to succeed.

"There's something wrong with this organization," he announced at a MEChA gathering. "We live in a democracy. It seems to me that these meetings are long on rhetoric and short on action. We need to engage in activities that help people by recruiting students, communicating with other campuses, and helping each other with study groups."

Rubalcava claimed Antonio had designs to grab power in the organization. Surprised by his former supporter's vitriol Antonio dropped out of MEChA. Jeff Solinas defended his friend's pro-social, proactive desire to bring Chicano students into the health professions.

His former mentor's baseless attack underscored Antonio's doubts concerning his future. A chance meeting with bright, ambitious pre-med sophomore Kathy Bond provided the support he needed.

A Californian from Alamo in the Bay Area, Kathy's father, a successful physician, and her mother had a rancorous relationship. Life became difficult for the young woman in the chaotic household. She opted to leave home at the age of sixteen.

With her Spanish language skills Kathy volunteered with Amigos de las Americas a non-governmental organization that trained teenagers to provide health care and immunizations in Latin American countries. The NGO assigned her to the small village of San Juan Chamelco in the central highlands of Guatemala. Kathy hiked into mountains delivering immunizations to indigenous Mayan populations.

"I did emergency first aid and sutured someone up for the first time in my life," Kathy recalled.

After her volunteer month expired she returned to California and enrolled at U.C. Santa Cruz majoring in science with the goal of attending medical school. Kathy remembered the day she met the newly minted Santa Cruz freshman in the lunch line of Crown College cafeteria.

University of California Santa Cruz, 1971. Antonio at Crown College. (Velasco Family Archive)

"Antonio was quiet and made an effort to talk to me. I was impressed because half the time no one would say anything. I mentioned that Gordon Lightfoot was appearing in concert and Antonio asked me if I wanted to go with him.

It was only later that I found out he had no idea who Gordon Lightfoot was."

His need to be accepted endeared Antonio to Kathy. However his pro-social views as well as his intellect drew her closer to him. She knew Antonio had a falling out with MEChA over the organization's philosophy. Kathy suggested that his Spanish language skills and focus on science would be a great asset at a farmworker clinic in Watsonville, California eighteen miles south of Santa Cruz.

Farms in the area supplied the United States with strawberries, apples, and lettuce and had a large population of Hispanic field hands. With his fluent Spanish and English Antonio became a valuable resource translating for health care providers who worked *pro bono* at the clinic.

The physician in charge of the clinic invited Antonio to join his research team. "Dr. Nitzberg the head of the University of California Santa Cruz Health Clinic arranged classes for every student who assisted him at the clinic. I also translated for Dr. Nitzberg, wrote diagnostic reports, studied medical charts and joined in with discussions about patients. That's when I knew I could do it," Antonio said in retrospect.

Emerging from farmworker culture Antonio identified that symptoms often presented by patients appeared to be the result of folk magic. Many of them suffered from a belief that a person with bad intentions cast *mal de ojo*, the Evil Eye, on them. The cure depended on psychological insight and the administration of placebos.

"I began to understand I had the ability to make diagnoses. Medicine was my future," said Antonio.

Kathy focused on interpreting for patients insuring they felt welcome at the clinic. Throughout this period they grew

108

closer. He was different from other students at Santa Cruz, the university known throughout the state as marching to the beat of its own drum exemplified by a nine-inch bright yellow organism with brown spots indigenous to Redwood forests surrounding Santa Cruz: the Banana Slug school mascot.

"He had been a farmworker and was interested in helping people. He didn't party like others at school. He remained focused on getting an education. Antonio was considerate, romantic, caring but above all he was charismatic," said Kathy.

To her dismay when Antonio entered his mother and father's home his perspective took a one-hundred-eighty-degree turn. "The men, including Antonio, expected women in his family to wait on them hand and foot. I considered myself a liberated woman and was surprised at the change in his attitude."

Kathy sensed his cultural mores ran much deeper than she imagined. Perhaps Antonio didn't recognize it consciously. A few instances in their relationship underlined difficulties she might face in their relationship. Antonio grew irate when she received letters from friends or when a male student talked with her.

Shortly after the visit to his parents' home they separated. Kathy returned for another stint in Guatemala before the start of the new semester. Antonio opted to continue school through summer and with Jeff Solinas searched for an outlet focusing on students from farm worker families.

Chicanos in Health Education (CHE) had been established in 1972 as an outgrowth of the National Chicano Health Organization. Its stated purpose was to bring qualified Latino students interested in science and health care into the university system. Chapters spread rapidly from the University of California, Berkeley throughout California.

Out-going, sociable, pre-med student Jeff Solinas and pragmatic detail oriented Antonio Velasco laid the groundwork to organize a chapter of CHE at U.C. Santa Cruz. It focused on academic support and gathering information about pre-medical courses and opportunities for minorities. When news reached Rubalcava that a nascent competing Hispanic organization might find a home on campus he attempted to blockade its request for official university credentials.

Jeff and Antonio adapted the CHE program for the specific needs of the Santa Cruz campus and presented it to the university administration. The dean and science faculty approved the plan over Rubalcava's objections. The university newspaper City on a Hill announced the official formation of the chapter with the headline "CHE To Unify Chicanos Interested in Health Fields."

The article quoted Antonio: *"I saw the need was there,"* *says Crown College sophomore Antonio Velasco, "and that's why* *CHE was formed...The need is for Chicanos to work together as a* *cohesive group, tutoring when necessary...There is information to* *be gathered as to the different academic and financial programs of* *the university, state, and junior college campuses, concerning the* *medical and health science programs...We would like to establish* *a liaison between neighboring high schools and colleges that do* *not have organizations such as CHE, or help them form their own* *group."*[50]

CHE To Unify Chicanos Interested In Health Fields

BY GARY KITAHATA
Staff Writer

"I saw the need was there," says Crown College sophomore Antonio Velasco, "and that's why CHE was formed." CHE means Chicanos for Health Education, and the organization was started by Antonio this quarter to unify all La Raza interested in the health fields.

"The need is for Chicanos to work together as a cohesive group, tutoring when necessary," quoted Velasco from the group's official Statement of Intention as a registered UC organization. "There is information to be gathered as to the different academic and financial programs of the university, state, and junior college campuses, concerning the medical and health sciences professions."

This information is not restricted to the Santa Cruz campus. "We would like to establish a liason between neighboring high schools or colleges that do not have organizations such as CHE, or help them form their own group," said Velasco.

Another goal of CHE is to work in community projects, such as the clinic in Berkeley staffed by CHE members at that UC campus. "The Cowell Extramural Program sends pre-med volunteers to a Comprehensive Health Clinic in South Carolina," Velasco explained. "We'd like to set up something like that at Alviso." Alviso is a Chicano community just outside of San Jose.

Anyone interested in CHE should contact Antonio Velasco at Crown College, Vox 459.

City on a Hill, UC Santa Cruz newspaper, Nov. 6, 1972. (Velasco Family Archive)

The day after the story appeared Richard Nixon won the election and entered his second term as President of the United States. Almost immediately the Senate Judiciary Committee began holding hearings about an illegal break-in of Democratic headquarters at the Watergate complex in

Washington, D.C. Suspicion of wrongdoing fell on Nixon.

The hearings demonstrated the strength of democracy and the rule of law. They also provided an impetus for CHE to continue battling for the right of minorities to higher education.

News of Chicano Health Education's success pushed Roberto Rubalcava to thwart the newly authorized group that attracted a small core of Latinas and Latinos from a variety of disciplines on campus. Against Rubalcava's protestations the university registrar supported CHE's first foray to recruit high school students interested in the sciences with an emphasis on health issues.

Volunteers arranged meetings with graduating high school students in the Central Valley home to thousands of migrant farmworker families many of whom had been in California for generations without ever stepping foot on a college campus. Traveling in an ancient school bus from Bakersfield in the south to Redding four hundred and fifty miles north, CHE introduced Santa Cruz science programs to Chicano students who had the talent and intellect for higher education.

The CHE charter emphasized support programs to maintain students in the university system and promote academic success for educationally disadvantaged, first-generation college, and low-income students. Graduates of the CHE program were encouraged to return to their communities to assist the under-served.

The constant pressure of organizing CHE, working in the university lab, and attending class took its toll on Antonio. He needed to get away from the campus on weekends. An ad from a nearby ranch offered room and board for a part-time caretaker.

He boarded in a large cabin overlooking a scenic canyon reminding Antonio of the hills and mountains in the highlands of Mexico. The pastoral atmosphere exercising horses, herding goats and maintenance brought relief from the constant turmoil on campus.

Chapter Ten

El amor todo lo puede

Jeff Solinas met every weekday for lunch during the summer session in the Merrill College dining room with Antonio where they mapped out plans for CHE. One afternoon Antonio found an attractive dark-haired sociology major Isabel Guzmán at the table with Jeff.

Isabel recalled meeting Antonio. "He had a green canvas army backpack over his shoulder and kept looking at me. Jeff asked Antonio to go to the beach with us. All he could do was mumble a few words. Then he spoke up and said he was in the process of growing bacteria in a lab. I said: 'Have fun' and we left."

Antonio had a distinctly different romantic memory of their meeting. "Isabel was right about my backpack. It held all my books, papers, and organization charts for CHE. I must have looked like a typical harried student. However Isabel bowled me over. The first time I saw her she stood on the top step of the dining hall. Isabel wore a burgundy pantsuit, and had long, curly hair. The light from a window framed her as if she was ethereal. I thought that if this girl went out with me I would be very happy. I was miserable that I couldn't stay with her because of my work in the lab."

"I thought it was a convenient excuse," laughed Isabel recalling their first encounter. He met Isabel once more at a back-to-school dance for the Education Opportunity Program. "I was with a friend who was an anthropology major," Isabel said. "Antonio and I danced one time and separated. He was very handsome but quiet. I thought that was it. Three days later he showed up at my dorm ostensibly to see how I was doing with my classes."

Antonio invited Isabel to accompany him to a bachelor party even though he had no concept of what a bachelor party entailed. They dressed for a semi-formal affair and found themselves attending an all-male boisterous touch football game. The young couple beat a hasty retreat to the beach where they sat on a wall over-looking the ocean and talked for hours in the warm dark night watching the moon send glimmers of light over fluorescent waves.

Isabel and Antonio began a relationship built on mutual understanding and common backgrounds. Both came from immigrant farm-working families. They had worked in the fields until high school and entered college. The struggle to overcome their familial history drew them together. Isabel joined CHE concentrating on recruiting students from her home territory in the San Joaquin Valley.

Chicanos in Health Education grew rapidly and soon operated at full speed. The core group set out on another recruiting trip. At each stop Antonio told his personal story as an example that others could follow. No longer able to ignore the influx of new Hispanic students to CHE, Rubalcava agreed reluctantly to help Antonio enroll students at Santa Cruz.

While Antonio relished CHE's achievement his academic life suffered. In his sophomore year he faced a major obstacle with physical chemistry a discipline that relies on sophisticated mathematics.

"The midterm exam bowled me over. I received a dismal score. It was the worst I ever had in school. My name was second to the lowest," recalled Antonio.

The episode resurrected doubts and fears he lived with since crossing the border. Antonio overcame his distress with an intense regimen. He crammed, studied, and reviewed his work two and three times before turning in assignments.

"At the end of the semester it all made sense. I scored in the top twenty-five percent of my class. My teacher wrote a glowing evaluation," Antonio declared.

The university named him student director of Chicanos for Health Education as he entered junior year. The first pre-med program had fifteen students who endured a grueling six-week orientation course.

With Isabel's encouragement he successfully completed a microbiology class. His dedication and knowledge impressed his professor who asked Antonio to intern in his laboratory as a paid assistant. Detail-oriented work fed the young student's curiosity to investigate core medical issues.

He had the good fortune to meet James Coleman[51] a pre-med student active in African American affairs. They had an intense desire to engage in community medicine and helped organize a student movement to improve minority admission to medical school. In terms of their percentage in the state, Hispanic and Asian American students together with African Americans represented a much smaller proportion of the school population. Strict meritocratic admissions policies excluded almost all Hispanic and African American students.

Political incidents in California's Central and Salinas Valleys that would shape Antonio Velasco's future began to unfold. In 1973 United Farm Worker leader César Chávez recruited Bill Monning[52] a graduate of the University of San Francisco School of Law to establish the Legal Department of the Migrant Farm Unit in Salinas. One of his principal aides was Juan Martínez who specialized in socio-economic issues. Another was Paralegal Dana Kent[53] a student from Radcliffe College in Massachusetts. They focused mainly on the landmark case United Farm Workers vs. International Brotherhood of Teamsters.

The contract between grape growers and United Farm Workers expired in 1973 and the Teamsters moved into the breech. Growers gave the Teamsters the right to organize farmworkers who were members of the UFW. It set off a protracted civil and legal battle.

Concerned that Teamsters misrepresented the willingness of UFW members to change membership, a coalition of religious, civic and labor leaders conducted a poll of farm workers in the Coachella Valley. On April 10, 1973 they released their results. Seven hundred ninety-five workers preferred the UFW; 80 preferred the Teamsters; and 78 wanted no union whatsoever.

The report stated: "We wish to encourage the grape growers to take seriously the expressed wishes of their workers…and to continue to support the right of farmworkers to their own union."[54]

An article in the New York Times affirmed: "In two actions in Federal District Court, claiming massive damages and charging a conspiracy with employers, the United Farm Workers, led by César Chávez, has thrown down the gauntlet

117

to the International Brotherhood of Teamsters... When the United Farm Workers attempted in August 1970, to institute strikes and boycotts, the growers obtained injunctions based on a California law that was meant to prevent competing unions from victimizing an employer in a jurisdictional dispute.

"Last month, the California Supreme Court dissolved these injunctions because evidence showed the growers had selected the teamsters as the union they wanted to do business with, and that there was no evidence to show the field workers wanted to be represented by the teamsters... While the United Farm Workers were being restrained by the lower court orders, the growers originated and supported with heavy financial contributions an unsuccessful attempt in the November election to adopt a law that would have limited the ability of labor unions to organize agricultural field workers... A peace agreement between the two unions, negotiated two years ago, was pretty much in tatters even before Mr. Chávez and his associates filed their damage action against the teamsters' union yesterday...teamsters' union officials agreed to help the agricultural interests in an attempt to avoid unionization by the United Farm Workers, the complaint alleged. The plan, it was charged, was 'to insulate growers and shippers from strikes and boycotts from other labor organizations'.

"The complaint again tentatively set class damages at $28,440,000 and asked that they be trebled to $85,320,000."[55]

The success of CHE at the University of California Santa Cruz in 1973 continued as Antonio's key extra-curricular pursuit. His prime responsibility involved difficult courses that would lead CHE participants to medical school. Antonio's work in the microbiology lab earned him enough money to pay for school tuition. A subsidy from the Education Opportunity

Program paid for residence fees and provided funds for textbooks.

Isabel remained at his side while he prioritized his tasks. "I liked the idea that a group of students dedicated themselves to recruiting students who helped one another," she stated.

In the spring of that year Antonio wrote a proposal for a summer pre-med program. The Provost of Crown College Dr. Kenneth Thimann[56] approved the project. Thimann named Antonio director of the Crown College Summer Premed Program permitting it to receive grants from Student Services and the backing of the university president to organize transportation and programs that brought five hundred students from the Central Valley to Santa Cruz.

Jeff Solinas graduated from Santa Cruz and entered the University of Southern California Medical School. Antonio had one more year before he could apply to U.C. Davis Medical School. Davis' proximity to the burgeoning UFW movement and population of the underserved, including migrant farm workers, were key considerations.

Minority students had assurances that bias in education had been erased via Executive Order 10925 signed by President John F. Kennedy in 1961. It stated: "discrimination because of race, creed, color, or national origin is contrary to the Constitutional principles and policies of the United States." Combined with the Civil Rights Act signed into law by President Lyndon B. Johnson in 1964 they became guiding principles for schools at all levels including universities.

A bombshell disrupted those principles ten years later. In 1974 Alan Bakke, a white engineer, sued the University of California alleging that Davis Medical School's rejection of his application violated Title VI of the Civil Rights Act of 1964[57] and the Fourteenth Amendment's Equal Protection Clause.

In the case of *Regents of the University of California versus Bakke* Judge F. Leslie Manker, Superior Court of California, Yolo County found the program unconstitutional and in violation of Title VI, "no race or ethnic group should ever be granted privileges or immunities not given to every other race."[58]

Manker ordered the medical school to disregard race as a factor, and to reconsider Bakke's application under a race-free system. Reverberations from the court case resounded across the entire education establishment.

The brunt of the decision fell on students of color. Disturbed but undeterred by the lower court's decision, Antonio worked on expanding Chicanos in Health Education. Minority students believed that as the Bakke case moved through the court system, the Supreme Court of California, a liberal bastion of civil rights, would reverse the lower court ruling.

Despite Roberto Rubalcava's agreement to help enroll students in Chicanos in Health Education animosity festered between MEChA and CHE. Rubalcava insisted on having input into all Chicano positions on campus. Still smarting over Jeff and Antonio's intrusion on his territory he interfered with Rita Solinas' application for the position of campus psychologist. Rubalcava wrote a letter to the provost and chancellor opposing Rita Solinas on the basis that she had an Italian surname. In his opinion the position should have been offered to someone with a Spanish name.

Antonio responded indignantly to Rubalcava. "That's the kind of petty politics in which you engage. Rita Solinas is a Chicana who married an Italian. It doesn't matter. Both Rita and George Solinas work with César Chávez. They're part

120

of the Chicano movement." Over Rubalcava's objections U.C. Santa Cruz appointed Rita Solinas as campus psychologist.

At CHE's education conference for welcoming new students Rubalcava set up a station at the door of the conference in an attempt to enroll students in MEChA. In a rebuke to his effort to defame Rita Solinas, who had become one of the most popular and respected members of the university staff and faculty, Antonio requested she give the keynote address at the convocation.

The meeting was the last major event Antonio held before entering his senior year in 1975. He continued working in the microbiology laboratory and organized the next pre-med program for CHE. Isabel remained at Santa Cruz working in the university cafeteria during the summer. Prior to the start of the fall semester Isabel and Antonio rented a small apartment off-campus and settled into domestic tranquility broken by an unexpected phone call from Antonio's paternal grandfather Jesús Velasco.

Unaware he had crossed the border and now lived in Los Angeles, Antonio exhibited anxiety that the volatile grandfather everyone feared wished to see him. On the three hundred fifty miles trip south they debated the pros and cons about bringing Jesús Velasco into their lives.

Antonio had been nine-years old when he last saw his grandfather. When they met in Los Angeles they discovered a gray-haired, thin man once feared as master of the world in Cofradía transformed into a mild-mannered elder.

Jesús insisted jealous family members invented tales about his rages. Whatever the truth, his grandfather had either reformed or tales of his extreme behavior had taken on legendary proportions. Jesús admitted pride in Antonio as the first in the family to attend a university. The old man moved into Antonio and Isabel's small apartment and found work at a flower nursery.

On one occasion Isabel's father, Heron Guzmán, visited and Jesús regaled everyone with stories about life in Mexico. "After hearing about Heron's cattle rancher father, my grandfather told him that he once had a herd. They were pigs. He had to take them from his village to another village a journey of two days. He spent the night in an arroyo where there was fresh water. In order to keep the pigs from straying he tied the chief pig to a tree, and they formed a circle around their leader. Heron asked Jesús 'Is all this true?' Jesús smiled for a moment then replied, 'Half of what I tell you is an exaggeration, the other half are lies.' He didn't say another word."

Antonio's grandfather moved to a small apartment in Davis and watched proudly as his grandson continued his education.

The end of the summer program brought a close to Isabel's job in the cafeteria. The professor who ran the microbiology lab where Antonio worked went on vacation. With the sudden lull in campus activity Antonio and Isabel fell back on their default position and found work picking apples in Watsonville. The job proved less strenuous than other fieldwork. In half a day they earned between eighty and a hundred dollars.

The students befriended the ranch foreman who asked Isabel to take on the additional task as his paid bookkeeper. From eight until ten in the morning she audited inventory. At ten she joined Antonio picking apples. By eleven in the morning they finished. It seemed ideal.

122

Another surprise call from Los Angeles announced that Antonio's cousin Lupio had arrived from Cofradía de Suchitlán as an undocumented worker in search of work. On the basis of his relationship with Antonio and Isabel the foreman hired Lupio.

Toward the end of the season he warned Isabel and Antonio that Lupio should not show up for work. Immigration authorities planned on making a major sweep of farms and orchards to roundup illegals for the purpose of abetting ranchers who withheld wages from undocumented workers. The cynical collusion between a branch of the government and ranchers incensed Antonio who was driven to battle discrimination in government and the private sector. Lupio subsequently abandoned fieldwork and became a specialist in dairy farming. Years later he became a successful electrician.

Chapter Eleven

Medical School

Second year medical student Antonio Ruelas,[59] actively engaged in Chicano activism during the 1960s and 70s, sat on the committee with Frank Meza.[60] In Southern California Ruelas joined Chicanos for Creative Medicine (CCM) that originated at East Los Angeles College in 1968.

Frank Meza, also with CCM, was active in Chicano affairs and a member of the Brown Berets, *Los Boinas Café* that fought for farm worker rights, education reform and against the Vietnam War. Ruelas and Meza became a formidable duo assisting Chicanos applying to Davis Medical. In 1969 only three Latinos enrolled in medical schools in California. CCM and other organizations came into existence to expand that universe. By 1974 the ranks of Hispanics in the medical professions grew exponentially.

Antonio and James Coleman scored identical high scores on the Medical College Admission Test (MCAT) in preparation for their application to medical school. The school accepted James while inexplicably, Antonio received a rejection letter.

His application crossed Ruelas and Meza's desks. Antonio's grades, extra-curricular lab work, and pro-social activities especially the formation of a CHE chapter at Santa

Cruz placed him in the top percentile of preferred students. To their dismay they found the school rejected the high scoring college student. The dean of the medical school assured the admissions committee no letters of rejection had been sent.

University California Davis Medical School (UC Davis Medical School)

The denial thrust Antonio back to high school when his bigoted counselor deliberately attempted to thwart his college application. Agitated over the denial he drove to Davis and confronted a secretary at the admissions office who informed him he did not qualify for admission because he was not a citizen. Antonio was due to receive his naturalization papers within fourteen days.

He researched entrance requirements for the University of California. They revealed citizenship was not a criterion. Eligibility solely depended on an appropriate Grade Point

Average and whether a person applying for admission was a resident of California. Antonio returned to Davis and demanded the school registrar accept him. The registrar reported no record of a rejection letter in his file.

Further investigation revealed that someone in the admissions office wrote the letter without authorization under the false assumption that applicants had to be citizens. The only copy of the document typed on UC Davis stationery was in Antonio's possession. Ruelas and Meza also uncovered the blunder. As a result, the Minority Admissions Committee invited Antonio for an interview. To his astonishment the first question his interviewer, a fourth-year medical student, asked was, "Are you a Chicano nationalist?"

Taken aback by the query, Antonio used it as an opportunity to convey his pride and point of view regarding minority rights and opportunities. "I am pro-Chicano. I believe society cannot progress as long as people remain oppressed. Everyone's position improves by bringing migrant farmworkers to universities and medical schools. However I do not believe I should progress by stepping on others. We're all in this together."

Years later Ruelas stated admiration for Antonio Velasco's intellect, pro-social consciousness, and genuine commitment to the farm worker community in California.

Antonio received his letter of admission to Davis. With almost obsessive dedication he set definitive goals checking them off in a journal he maintained through most of college and medical school and several years thereafter.

During his first year in medical school Antonio and Isabel took turns driving from Davis to Santa Cruz and back again. They promised Isabel's parents they would not marry until she graduated from college. The pressure of difficult courses and his desire to be with Isabel came into conflict. They decided to have their wedding in his second year of medical school, a few days after Isabel graduated from UC Santa Cruz.

Wedding picture: Isabel Guzman Velasco and Antonio Ramirez Velasco, 1976. (Velasco Family Archive)

Isabel's father insisted on a wedding that would accommodate not only the immediate family but their extended family as well. He expected many of them to travel from his home village of Jeruco in Michoacan, Mexico. They anticipated a minimum of one hundred guests. Antonio's family would make up a very small portion of those attending. After the wedding at St. Anne Catholic Church in Porterville they planned a return to Woodville for the reception in a banquet hall. The Guzmáns demanded the Velascos provide the feast. Although the cost of food seemed beyond their budget, José's dignity was at stake and he agreed.

In retrospect Herón Guzmán acted with an air of

authority learned from his father, a small cattle rancher. Jeruco was a poverty stricken village on Lake Cuitzeo where they measured prosperity by the size of one's herd.

For all his grandiosity, Herón had been a migrant farm worker. The Guzmáns and Velascos lived modest, hard-working lives. Typical of many immigrants, the legend of Herón's father grew larger every year. Ten head of cattle became a significant herd. Status had more to do with prestige and respect rather than money.

Teresa Velasco worked for days preparing food in the steamy kitchen of her home in Greenfield. The morning of the wedding José and Teresa loaded pots, pans and paper bags filled with food in the back of their pickup truck. They headed for Porterville, a three-hour drive south on Interstate 101 then east on narrow, curving California Highway 198.

The truck fitfully motored between vast fields of cotton, citrus orchards, and alfalfa. Halfway to their destination smoke erupted from the engine. The truck sputtered to a stop at the side of the road. With no homes in sight or access to a phone line, José dove under the hood to make repairs. Two hours later the Velascos headed for Woodville instead of the church in Porterville.

Historic mission-style St. Anne Catholic Church built in 1896 gleamed white under a bright summer sun. Two marble columns rose above the marble altar. Guests waited for José and Teresa Velasco in the flower-bedecked church before a nave that soared to a carved wood ceiling. After an hour the priest insisted he could wait no longer. A despondent Antonio went through the rites stoically. Compounding his embarrassment, Antonio had been unable to purchase a wedding ring for himself and had to borrow his brother-in-law's. After the

128

wedding everyone returned to Woodville for the reception with an impatient Heron Guzmán convinced the Velascos had reneged on their promise to supply the feast.

José called the reception hall from a service station and left a message that he and Teresa would soon arrive. The truck pulled into the parking lot with Teresa, her grease-covered husband and a truck loaded with pots and pans filled with a magnificent feast.

The newlyweds placed their honeymoon on hold until Isabel completed her Masters in Education. Antonio elected to take his third-year rotation at Natividad Medical Center in Salinas, one of the first medical institutions with a Family Medicine department and the same hospital that saved his mother's life years before.

Salinas, the home of John Steinbeck author of the seminal novel *The Grapes of Wrath* about migrant farmworkers and their plight during the tragic era of the Dust Bowl, became a testing ground for immigrant farmworker medical services, a task that Antonio saw as mandatory. Illnesses contracted in the fields or from lack of sanitation could impact the general public. It also gave the young intern who understood farmworker culture, folkways and spoke their language, an opportunity to engage and diagnose patients.

"I needed to decide my specialty by my third year. During my six-week rotation at Natividad I worked in surgery, obstetrics and gynecology, pediatrics, and family medicine," Antonio recalled.

He found a genial mentor in an affable activist resident Dr. Bruce Greenburg who organized the first program allowing medical students to perform rotations at Natividad. Dr. Greenburg also worked with the UFW to assist farmworkers with medical care at a time when difficulties arose concerning union elections between the farmworker union and Teamsters. During his first term as governor of California Jerry Brown appointed a pro-UFW Agricultural Labor Relations Board to supervise the election. The ALRB ran out of funding and suspended operations for five months until the state legislature voted for an appropriation.

The UFW suffered a major setback in November 1976 when Proposition 14 on the California ballot guaranteeing funding for the ALRB and free access to union organizers lost by a two-to-one margin. The event instigated division and dissent in the United Farm Worker staff. A few of Chávez's longtime associates believed he was not willing to delegate responsibility and acted like a dictator.[61]

By the time Antonio began his rotation a schism erupted between Natividad and the union's clinic when misdiagnosed patients showed up at the hospital. Antonio was appalled that the physician who ran the UFW clinic prescribed Librium[62] to almost every patient regardless of symptoms.

"I stopped my activity with the UFW clinic because it was harming patients. Either you were on the side of Natividad or the side of the clinic," Antonio stated.

César Chávez arrived at the medical facility for a physical and the physician prescribed Librium for no obvious medical reason or appropriate diagnosis. Visibly angry, Chávez immediately shut down the clinic leaving a breach in fieldworker medical care.

Farmworker health languished when the UFW failed to establish a new clinic in Salinas. Antonio organized a committee to start a community health center. They traveled to UFW headquarters in La Paz to meet with Chávez. The

130

UFW leadership expressed no interest in opening a clinic at the time.

Antonio asked Chávez what he thought was the major health problem facing farmworkers. Chávez replied: "pesticides pose the greatest risk to farmworkers." That stark comment returned to Antonio as he faced pesticide poisonings that erupted in the following years.

Antonio used time off to visit labor camps, sites that brought back vivid memories of working in fields under extreme duress. He suggested to Dr. Greenburg that migrant workers required medical assistance closer to their housing. An article published in UC Davis Medicine notes that Dr. Greenburg credits Antonio with convincing him to volunteer for the "needy at a nearby labor camp a couple of nights a week."[63]

Antonio and eleven of his colleagues signed up with Medi-Corps[64] funded by the Migrant Education Program. A team of three undergraduate students majoring in health-related careers worked in each of the forty-seven migrant labor camps throughout California under the supervision of residents and interns. Students provided physical exams for children and young adults.

Medi-Corps transferred Antonio to Buena Vista Migrant Center north of Watsonville, California. The largest labor camp in the state had a population of five-hundred-fifty farmworkers almost all of whom came from a village in Michoacan, Mexico. Its homogeneity enabled researchers to focus on genetic transmission of ailments.

Bruce Greenburg set up a temporary medical station providing blood pressure readings and delivering diabetes screenings. Three Medi-Corps workers signed up for Buena

Vista. One volunteer failed to participate. According to Antonio's journal, it created an overload on students. He felt that successful screening of children could not be accomplished unless he spent additional time at the camp. Buena Vista slowly evolved into a permanent health facility. Antonio won a grant that paid physicians and supported the center.

Completing his successful rotation at Natividad Antonio returned to Davis. Isabel and Antonio rented the second floor in a two level Victorian house in Sacramento. With her newly acquired Masters in Education Isabel gained a position with a migrant education program. She taught at a labor camp and summer sessions in a local school where she brought children from Mexico up to speed during the short time they were in the county. With her formidable skills Isabel created a program to assist migrant farm children break the cycle of camp-to-camp existence and realize their potential.

Antonio volunteered to work at *Clínica Tepati* a medical facility in Sacramento that gained prominence as the premier free health clinic in the area. Founded in 1974 by U.C. Davis professor Dr. Gabriel Smilkstein, the medical establishment provided hands on medicine to farm workers, immigrants and the vulnerable segment of the Latino community that could not afford to pay for adequate health care.

Dr. Smilkstein believed physicians in training and doctors in general needed to break the bonds forged by those in the medical profession who thought they had all the answers to the healing process.

Smilkstein wrote his theory that "...cultural medicine as practiced by family elders, priests, witch doctors, sorcerers, herbalists, and acupuncturists who are not physicians is scorned by professionals in western medicine.

132

Yet the supportive role played by these traditionalists serves to meet many of the anxieties and concerns generated by ill health. Most of these anxieties and concerns are poorly understood by western doctors because the doctors function outside the patients' cultural milieu... healing is a multidimensional phenomenon which includes not only the classical psychosomatic factors, but also the ethical and cultural elements of the patient's lifestyle...Translators must be found ... who can interpret the ethical and cultural needs of the...residents to those delivering medical assistance. These translators will also function to reassure the... community of the role which will be played by outside professionals. Communication... is essential but equally important is the need to train health workers to perform effectively outside the sphere of an upper middle-class socio-economic pattern from which most health workers come."[65]

In his first year Antonio was nominated director-elect designee. He continued working at *Clínica Tepati* in his second year. He went on to serve in the Sacramento County Clinic that operated weekdays in the same neighborhood. The two facilities had no mutual relationship a situation Antonio set about to resolve. He and Frank Meza wrote a proposal to the County Director of Public Health suggesting they work as one entity.

"We would provide bilingual medical services at no cost to Sacramento County. In turn they provided the facility with all the medical supplies necessary," said Antonio. "The proposal was simple. We could join together in order to provide medical services six days a week. *Clínica Tepati* would become an integral part of the county health system and have access to full-time examining rooms with all the supplies necessary to carry out our mandate of providing quality medical care," Antonio responded.

The county Director of Public Health prepared a working agreement. The summer between Antonio's first and second year of medical school the clinic became a full-time operation.

"I return to the clinic now and then," reminisced Antonio. "Today it provides not only medical services, but also dentistry and outreach programs. When medical students recognize my name they're surprised I'm still alive. I feel like a dinosaur but very proud of the clinic's success."

Time permitting, Antonio drove south two hundred fifty-miles to visit Isabel who remained at U.C. Santa Cruz. On breaks in her schedule she reciprocated and joined Antonio in Davis where she stayed with him in a small apartment he rented with James Coleman.

The intense activism for students of color placed a mental and physical burden on Antonio. To escape the pressure after completing their final exams he and James Coleman decided on the spur of the moment to travel to Ensenada, Mexico in Baja California without informing Isabel.

They packed up their meager belongings along with a piece of salami and bags of chips and piled into James' black and gold Pontiac Firebird Trans Am. The moment they crossed the border a major thunderstorm battered the peninsula. Pelting rain turned the arid desert into a muddy swamp. Streams and rivers burst out of dry arroyos and flooded roads.

Resolved to brave the deluge they decided to cruise the entire length of the peninsula. Rain eased up and they found themselves on a narrow road with water-filled potholes the size of bathtubs. On each side eerie Boojum trees grew to heights of seventy feet in a stark landscape of Yucca and Cardon cactus.

134

They jounced down the road for two hours until they saw police stopping cars. Making a rapid diagnosis that it was a shakedown for money, James swiftly made a U-turn and beat a hasty retreat north. They bought bongo drums as souvenirs in Tijuana and crossed the border into the United States. That night they camped on a San Diego beach slapping and banging on the bongos until they fell asleep in the safety of California.

Angry and upset that Antonio failed to inform her about his sudden urge to take off on an adventure Isabel threatened to leave him unless he pulled himself together. Contrite and apologetic, Antonio promised to change his ways.

Political turmoil on campus over Bakke consumed Antonio. "If you are brown, or black, or a woman, or an Asian it really counts against you when you apply to medical school," Antonio said in a *San Francisco Chronicle* article The program at Davis helped ameliorate the situation however "we are having problems." He felt "very intimidated by the faculty, and overt racism in the school."[66]

Memo from Dr. Donal Walsh to Dr. Ernest Gardner, Davis Medical College, 1975. "The impact of task force [minority] students on the curriculum". (Velasco Family Archive)

In 1975 Dr. Donal Walsh a member of the Executive Committee of the Davis Faculty wrote a memo titled *"The impact of task force students on the curriculum."* It intimated institutional bias toward minority medical students. Addressed to Ernest Gardner, M.D., Chairman of the Committee on Educational Policy (CEP) at Davis, Walsh expressed his concerns about "task force students" i.e. minority students, in the medical program.

136

"By the introduction of task force students into the student body, we have invalidated this mechanism of determination of quality [*statistical analysis as a criterion of establishing the passing grade*]...the presence of task force students has resulted in...a decreased passing grade and a resultant pass for several task force and non-task-force students that should not otherwise have qualified...The medical school has introduced students on an experimental basis, immediately de facto defined them as uniform and equivalently qualified to other students, and thus automatically given most a passing grade. To emphasize a point by reducing it to the absurd—if we had introduced twenty first grade students into the medical school class many of them would still have received grades within the resultant two standard deviations of the mean...

"...I would request that the CEP's [*Committee on Education Policy*] evaluation of the effect of task force students on the curriculum would include 1) a reevaluation of our method of establishing the passing grade of examinations, 2) a determination of whether the presence of task force students has lowered the mean and increased the standard deviation of examination results, and 3) an evaluation of whether this has on its face resulted in an increased pass rate for task force students."[67]

Dr. Gardner forwarded the Walsh memo to Course Managers and Department and Division Chairman with the following note: "Dr. Lois O'Grady, at the request of the Executive Committee has asked the Committee on Educational Policy to consider the impact of Task Force Students on our curriculum and on student performance. The question has been asked: Are we downgrading our curriculum and expecting

137

less of 85% of our students so that 8% can pass? The Executive Committee has also asked that in our deliberations we query Course Committee chairmen to see if this question has any validity in fact.

"There is also a question about grading. We tend to use a standard deviation type approach flunking those students who fall below two standard deviations. However, if there is a group of students who are consistently below the rest of the class, this will drag down the standard deviation and affect the scores of the entire class. I am enclosing a copy of a memorandum from Dr. Donal Walsh, in which he expresses concern about the impact of task force students on the curriculum and outlines the nature of the problem.

"I would appreciate hearing from you about whether or not a statement that we are downgrading our curriculum has any validity. What is the impact of Task Force methods? Are there any other criteria that can be used?"[68]

San Francisco Chronicle, Nov. 18, 1976. "Medical Students Examine Minority Program" (Velasco Family Archive)

138

The memo surfaced in 1976 and Antonio wrote a scathing article for the publication *Inside UC Davis* claiming racial discrimination on campus. His article placed a label on Antonio as a troublemaker. Minority students teachers as well as Davis administrators who supported students of color in their quest to become health care provider, supported Antonio's viewpoint.

Chapter Twelve

El Corazón de Antonio

The National Chicano Health Organization (NCHO) closed shop after its final meeting in 1976 at U.C. Davis Medical School when it failed to gain federal funding. The loss of NCHO created a void for continuing support of Latino medical education. A committee led by Antonio, José Alberto Arévalo, University of California, Berkeley, Jeff Solinas, University of Southern California Medical School, and Stanford medical student Loretta Ortiz y Piño[69] structured a financially viable framework for the purpose of recruiting and providing funds and programs for Latino medical students.

Their plan came at a critical time. The Bakke case moved to the California Supreme Court. Expectations ran high in the Latino community that it would reject the lower court ruling. In what many considered a betrayal of principles, Judge Stanley Mosk handed down an unexpected verdict on September 16, 1976 upholding the lower court's decision.

Mosk wrote: "…no applicant may be rejected because of his race, in favor of another who is less qualified, as measured by standards applied without regard to race."[70]

Davis shut down its quota system and appealed to the U.S. Supreme Court. University of California San Francisco students protested the California court's decision and organized the Alliance for Responsible Employment and Admissions.

140

They released a statement that expressed the views of most minority students as well as white students who looked upon the Bakke decision as a major step backward in the fight for civil rights, equity, and justice.

"The Bakke decision must be viewed within the context of its historical development and contemporary setting. Affirmative action programs represent minimal victories in the fight against discrimination. These gains are now threatened. In a period of high unemployment and economic cutbacks, poor and working whites and people of color are placed in direct competition with each other for too few training opportunities, jobs and services. As more and more middle class Americans join the ranks of the unemployed.

"...the arrogant assumption that people of color admitted and employed through affirmative action programs are 'less qualified' than other applicants. This assumption must be attacked as must be the equally arrogant assumption that criteria based upon the skill, standards, and norms of white middle class culture reflect a higher intelligence.

"We reject the cultural and racial bias of these employment and admissions standards and demand the development of alternative criteria which confront head-on the reality of discrimination.

"Born out of the false confidence that the violent energies of the past decade have been pacified, the Bakke Decision is one more distorted reflection in the mirror of contemporary social thinking.

"Along with massive cutbacks in health, education and welfare spending and the directing of the gross national product toward the defense budget to offset the international rise to power of Third World Nations.

"The California High court heralded as the most progressive in the country has struck a direct blow at the affirmative action gains made in the last ten years."[71]

The decision offered an incentive to develop the successor to the defunct National Chicano Health Organization. The committee that met at the NCHO conference received a grant from the Federal Bureau of Health Professions[72] to organize La Raza Medical Association, La RaMA, a new, progressive Latino student medical group in 1977. It elected Jeff Solinas as its first president.

The grant provided La RaMA $125,000 per year for three years. They built a staff to identify and support pre-med students that did not have the financial means to pay tuition. Hispanic medical students rallied around the new entity.

La RaMA selected Antonio and Jeff Solinas from the University of Southern California Medical School to attend the American Medical Students Association (AMSA)[74] conference in New Orleans. They believed a partnership with AMSA would heighten the nascent organization's credibility.

They cornered the incoming president of AMSA Charlie Clements[74] for assistance. Clements, an Air Force veteran who flew transport aircraft in Vietnam became a vocal opponent of the war and refused to fly further missions when he witnessed the illegal bombing of the neighboring nation of Cambodia.

142

Charlie Clements, MD. (C. Clements)

The Air Force viewed his refusal to fly after a career as an accomplished pilot who attained the rank of captain as a form of psychosis and committed him to a psychiatric hospital. He was given a medical discharge in 1971. Clements returned to the United States and held a variety of jobs as a crewman on yachts and tramp steamers. He taught physics at the University of the South Pacific in Fiji and worked on rural development projects in India.

Eventually he attended the University of Washington Medical School where he received his medical degree and opted to earn a Master of Public Health. Clements was elected president of the American Medical Students Association and served through 1980.

During the time Antonio spent with Clements and his significant other Julie Hurlocker, also a graduate of the

University of Washington Medical School, in New Orleans they bonded over their passion for social justice.

The Latino community experienced rapid growth in California. In 1970 Hispanics numbered twelve percent of the state's population. By 1976 it increased to nineteen percent approaching twenty representing over four million individuals.

However they remained underrepresented in the state's medical schools. La RaMA set out to increase Hispanic enrollment in the health professions.

The organization held its first conference at Davis, the epicenter of the battle over medical school minority rights. Dr. José Alberto Arévalo stated in an interview that the presentation by Antonio Velasco and Antonio Ruelas describing the *Clínica Tepati* program was one of the conference highlights.

With the assistance of La RaMA the *Clínica Tepati* model that afforded educational opportunities for medical students gained strength and eventually became an integral part of the Davis medical curriculum. Those who worked at the clinic received benefits from "transcript notation." Credits on official transcripts were based on participation in the medical facility of at least forty hours per quarter, internship titles, organization, and quarters served.

The clinic officially documented university-approved internships and conveyed extracurricular activities to prospective graduate schools and employers. Transcript notation also assisted medical students establish goals with internship supervisors. Eventually it became a course in the medical school.

The success of the clinic and encouragement for the support of minority students had a major impact on college campuses throughout the nation. Medical schools across the United States adopted the *Clínica Tepati* paradigm confirming the efficacy of Latinos in the health care system.

Dr. Arévalo saw a quiet dynamism in Antonio that transformed a young, unassuming medical student into one whose passion for medicine and love of social justice came together. "The hallmark of someone like Antonio," said Dr. Arévalo, "was the ability to inspire others. We called it *el corazón de Antonio* (Antonio's heart) that became *el corazón de las estudiantes* (the students' heart)."

Rallies protesting the Bakke decision erupted organically on college campuses culminating in one of the largest gatherings with a teach-in Friday, Feb. 25, 1977 at Sproul Hall, U.C. Berkeley. The following month CHE sponsored a conference about the Bakke Decision at the University of California, San Francisco. It addressed the need to look at the possibilities of future programs in light of the California State Supreme Court's decision and how the U.S. Supreme Court might rule in the pending appeal.

Synapse, the UC San Francisco student newspaper reported: "...minorities are underrepresented in public health schools. (According to California State Department of Health Statistics, minorities represent twenty-six per cent of the state, yet there were only 15.5 per cent minority students in 1975-76 entering classes in medical schools in the state); there are not enough minority physicians in the country; (of the estimated 357,000 practicing physicians in the U.S., approximately 2.2 per cent are Black although the nation's 25 million Blacks represent twelve per cent of the population. Chicanos comprise 5 million (2.5 per cent of the population) but only an estimated 250 Chicanos are practicing physicians.

"There is a serious need for improved health care in minority communities; —minority students do return to practice in their communities after graduation; —minority students admitted under special programs are doing well and many are not 'less qualified' than those admitted under traditional standards...traditional admissions criteria, such as Medical College Admissions Tests (MCAT) scores and grade point averages are not fair indicators of how a student, especially minority, will do in school or how a good doctor he/she may become.

"Although the State Supreme Court did rule that special admissions programs based solely on the basis of race are unconstitutional, the Court did clearly support special efforts to serve disadvantaged students... the Court did propose alternative methods of reaching the goals of special admissions programs. Among them were: modifying regular admission standards, taking away the large emphasis on MCATs and GPAs and putting more consideration into personal interviews, and applicant's professional goals; also modifying special programs providing preferential treatment to 'disadvantaged' students provided no applicant is rejected because of his/her race.

"Peter Roos of the Mexican American Legal Defense Fund said that it is important to define 'disadvantaged' so that if it does become a part of special admissions criteria it insures sufficient representation of minority students.

"Assemblyman John Vasconcellos (D-San José) urged people to take relevant information and present it to legislators so they can become more aware of it. He said that every State legislator and administrator should be seen by students and concerned citizens and asked what they are doing to make sure affirmative action programs are working.

"Vasconcellos, Chairman of the Assembly Permanent Committee on Postsecondary Education, held hearings in Sacramento yesterday on the Bakke decision and the issue or increasing access for disadvantaged graduate students.

"Assemblyman Art Torres (Dem.-L.A.) said programs are not going to be implemented on their own and one can't always depend on university administrators. Both [Vasconcellos and Torres] said that the Student Legislature cannot determine UC policy, but it can influence it because it does control the amount of allocation to the University.

"One attorney suggested a letter writing campaign to Griffin Bell and President Carter's administration urging it to file a brief to the U.S. Supreme Court in defense of special admissions programs.

"Mario Obledo, Secretary to the State Health and Welfare Agency said that there are sympathetic people in the State administration. But these people need to know the facts and the information that could give them a push to do something.

"Cruz Reynosa, Associate Justice of the Third Appellate Court of California, said…no matter what the Courts rule, the fight for affirmative action should continue. 'Affirmative action programs are right,' he said. 'Let's do what we think is right because it's right, not because the Supreme Court says yes or no.'"[75]

Chapter Thirteen

The First Campaign

During the Bakke upheaval Isabel became pregnant shifting Antonio's priorities to his wife and the impending birth of their first child. Although an accomplished and well-respected obstetrician he was overcome by anxiety. Fearing his emotional empathy might cloud his judgment he turned Isabel's care over to another physician.

Throughout the eight months Antonio leaned into Isabel's expanding abdomen talking to the unborn child and feeling it kick with what he believed were responses to his voice. Isabel went into the hospital on November 21, 1978. Although she had a difficult labor the baby was born without incident.

"Anisvel arrived and was beautiful like a cherub," Antonio said. "In that moment I felt I met someone I already knew and with whom I had a connection. The nurse placed the baby on Isabel's belly. I held Anis and kissed her. It was a magic time. After half-an-hour I decided to go the cafeteria. As I walked to the door Anisvel began to cry. I talked to her and she stopped crying. It seemed coincidental. I went out to the corridor and she cried once more only to stop when I returned. I felt a strong connection with my daughter that still exists."

If the birth of Anisvel and the wellbeing of Isabel remained at the top of his agenda, completing medical school ran a close second. Antonio entered his last year of medical school along with James Coleman. They did their last rotation at the Veterans Administration Hospital in Martínez, California one hundred-ten-miles southwest of Davis.

Isabel and Antonio could not afford another move and he had no desire to be separated from his wife and Anis. Every day during a bleak and miserable winter he and James made the round trip leaving at four-thirty in the morning to arrive for rounds at six. When they returned home he spent late nights preparing write-ups on the day's activities.

The VA hospital housed veterans of World War Two many of whom were terminal. In the 21st century monitors measure the majority of patients' physiology. In 1978 blood samples were taken every four hours and analyzed manually by residents in a dank, remote basement laboratory.

At the end of their rotation at the VA, supervising interns gave Antonio and James disappointingly modest evaluations. After mid-quarter and final exams they scored 3.0, the standard minimum for a passing grade the previous quarter. Without notification to the student body Davis administration changed the passing score to 3.45. The sudden deviation in the passing grade point average appeared arbitrary.

Antonio rebelled over what he deemed a capricious and covert decision to change passing grades by a fraction that primarily affected minority medical students. The incident resulted in an invitation to speak about minority discrimination in post-graduate education at a major rally held in Berkeley California headlined by African American activist Angela Davis and Native American advocate Dennis Banks.

His reputation as a University of California, Davis agitator shot to the top of the list. The school ordered Antonio and James Coleman to repeat their rotation in internal medicine. Fed up with Davis' vacillating proposal to change scores without notification, James opted to complete his residency elsewhere.

Antonio refused to leave Davis out of concern for Isabel and Anis. He flashed back to feelings of frustration and anguish over what he believed was a deliberate ploy to eliminate students who entered medical school under the minority admissions program. "It was do-or-die for me. Isabel saw how hard I worked at the VA hospital that winter. She knew I received a passing evaluation and had decent grades on the exams. It was a low point in my education."

The discovery of the memo written in 1975 by Dr. Donal Walsh a member of the Executive Committee of the Davis Faculty claiming that Task Force [minority] Students lowered standards supported Antonio's assertion that it represented a political not academic decision.

"I thought the school misinterpreted its mission. Davis declared its goal was training primary care physicians who would serve the community with compassion. Support of that mission seemed to be lacking at the time."

Antonio presented evidence that the new standards attempted to weed out students of color. In order to avoid a protracted battle that could become a *cause celebre* in the media, the administration and Antonio reached a compromise on the repeat of his rotation. Instead of the usual twelve-week rotation he was allowed to take a six-week program. Residents and doctors had a keen awareness that Antonio's skills far exceeded his scores on paper. The compromise regarding his

150

rotation did not diminish Antonio's concern for the wellbeing of minority students.

The school appointed a faculty physician to supervise and act as sole arbiter of Antonio's progress. Observation and written evaluations determined success or failure. After repeating his rotation Davis granted Antonio his medical degree.

The 1979 Davis School of Medicine graduating class recognized his leadership and tenacity and overwhelmingly elected Antonio to deliver the commencement address. José Dolores Velasco, the father who derided Antonio for believing that the child of a farmworker could aspire to a higher calling, attended the ceremony with his wife, Teresa, sisters and brother.

Antonio's passionate address encompassed his philosophy of social justice and health care working hand-in-hand. In part he said: "Primary and preventive health care are acute needs in our society. Rural areas, in general, have problems attracting physicians, as do poor inner-city areas, ghettos, and barrios.

"We must recognize that health isn't just physical and thus we must strive to change the social and educational conditions that help perpetuate the current status of the population we are serving. We must step out of the examination room and deal with community problems and practice a medicine which is aimed at improving the health status of the population as a whole, not just an individual who pays for a doctor's visit."

The dean of the medical school whispered to Antonio he had never seen a father so proud of his son as José Velasco. Acceptance of his achievements from José matched Antonio's triumph over the never-ending harvest cycle when he entered the world of science and healing.

Natividad's Family Medical Practice Department accepted Antonio as one of six out of five hundred and fifty applicants. The hospital's migrant farm base provided physicians opportunities to treat pathologies rarely seen in other facilities.

Immediately after receiving his medical license the United States Supreme Court announced a victory for civil rights in America. By a five to four vote the court in Regents of the University of California v. Bakke upheld affirmative action for admitting students to the university. It made the taxing work of seeing nine patients a day during a three-hour period at Natividad slightly less onerous and resolved a major issue for minority students.

The positive, affirming decision gave Antonio a breather. He made a tough decision to open a private practice aimed at expanding services to migrant farmworkers. Natividad did not want to lose the skilled physician. In return for retaining his practice within the confines of the medical facility the hospital provided two exam rooms, a nurse and receptionist for four hours a day, four days a week.

Nurse's Aide Dora Alonzo joined him in his private practice as a volunteer. Another nurse's aide came aboard as a volunteer as well. According to a UCSC Review article published a year later, Antonio, Luisa Buada, RN 76 and Randy Alto a registered nurse training as a physician's assistant at Stanford University had misgivings that after the shutdown of the UFW clinic in Salinas in November 1978 over twelve-thousand migrant and seasonal farmworkers would have minimal primary health care.

A grant from the California State Department of Health provided seed money to physicians who agreed to practice in underserved communities and rural areas. With friends and acquaintances from U. C. Santa Cruz, Jeff Solinas and attorney Lydia Villareal, nurses Buada and Alto visited clinics and met with prospective patients throughout the state in order to determine necessary requirements to secure superior health care for farmworkers who did not have access to adequate medical services.

Antonio's determined efforts moved beyond medicine to workers' rights and their fight for collective bargaining with growers. Individually farm workers had no power to coerce changes in working conditions and wages. United, workers who supplied the marketplace with fresh produce could earn a living wage thus making a major difference in their lives and the lives of their families. Higher wages benefitted not only workers. An increase in buying power and taxes supported the general welfare.

The United Farm Workers engaged in a battle with the Salinas Marketing Co-op and other large agribusinesses in the Salinas and Imperial Valleys over a collective bargaining agreement that had expired in late 1978.

Antonio gathered signatures, assisted with petitions, and helped marshal resources for the UFW. In the midst of the organizing effort he met Bill Monning, the dynamic young attorney who formed the Legal Department of the Migrant Farm Unit in Salinas for the UFW in 1978. The following year Monning joined California Rural Legal Assistance (CRLA) and staffed an office in Salinas where Dana Kent, now his wife, taught bilingual education at San Juan Bautista Elementary School.

CRLA, a non-partisan, apolitical organization concentrated on poverty law and the welfare of farmhands and others who could not afford to hire attorneys when conflicts arose between workers and employers. The stated mission of CRLA is to fight for justice and individual rights alongside the most exploited communities of society.

With an advisory committee of farmworkers Monning inaugurated the Migrant Farmworker Unit of CRLA in Salinas. They identified four key areas in which to become involved: health, education, labor rights, and housing. Monning focused on pesticide litigation and advocacy.

The UFW and farm operators came to loggerheads over the attempt by the Teamsters Union to represent farmworkers. Eventually it came before the State of California Agricultural Board. It adjudicated the case on behalf of the UFW's right to[77] negotiate collective bargaining agreements with growers.

Moving between the union-grower battle and the hospital, Antonio, Jeff Solinas, attorney Lydia Villareal, Luisa Buada and Randy Alto formed *Clínica Popular* a private, non-profit corporation to serve farmworkers. Personnel at *Clínica* had anecdotal information that farm workers suffered disproportionately from debilitating illnesses. Many in the migrant farm worker population were undocumented therefore accurate studies did not exist.

The National Migrant Referral Project[78] bolstered Antonio's campaign to administer health care to farmworkers. The Health Policy Institute, Boston University, published documented research that farm workers, including those in California, suffered higher rates of respiratory problems caused by pesticides and fungicides.

"…the occupational and associated living conditions

154

of migrant and seasonal agricultural workers in the U.S. pose exceptional health hazards to the workers and their dependents...The extremely negative health consequences of farmworker living conditions...Adequate solutions for this impoverished and powerless group...will require significant sociopolitical advances such as unionization and other forms of political organization."[79]

Clínica Popular was jubilant when they received word of a two hundred-thousand-dollar federal grant. The sweet taste of celebration swiftly turned sour. The grant was frozen when President Jimmy Carter failed to rally support for his programs. The Republican controlled 96th Congress, emboldened by the passage in California of Proposition 13[80] took austerity measures to new heights. The Farmworkers Health Services Unit of the California Department of Health filled the void and provided the clinic with two hundred twenty thousand dollars to open its doors.

"By word of mouth we found out about a building at 122 N. Main St., Salinas," said Luisa Buada. "It had originally been a lodging house, but it needed a lot of renovation to bring it up to code for use as a clinic."

The construction crew that built George Solinas' Philippine farmworker retirement center, Agbayani Village, in Delano, California converted the cottage. The dining room became the reception area; the kitchen and breakfast room were rebuilt as a dispensary and laboratory. Four bedrooms were remodeled as examining rooms.

Antonio became medical director of the clinic. He recruited Jon Andrus from U.C. Davis who trained at Santa Rosa County Medical Center and Larry Bruguera a resident at Stanislaus Medical Center in Merced, California. Dana Kent volunteered to raise funds for Antonio's *Clínica Popular.*

"We were paid for our work at Natividad and volunteered our time at the clinic," recalled Antonio. "Day-to-day operations were taken care of by Workers Compensation paid by the state for farmworker injuries and work-related illnesses."

In 1980 Dana Kent and Bill Monning expected their first child. To their misgiving the doctor who cared for her went on vacation at the time the baby was due. Antonio was called to the delivery room where Monning reported he helped tamp down their distress about the absent physician and attended at the delivery of a healthy baby girl. The event cemented their relationship. Monning and Kent continued their support of Clinica Popular.

In 1981 the clinic changed its name to *Coalición de Salud para el Valle de Salinas* (Health Coalition for the Salinas Valley).[81] It evolved over four decades into a major health care system.

"Today it operates seven clinics throughout Monterey County and provides for two-hundred patients a year," reported Antonio. "It also provides comprehensive services that include outpatient care, obstetrical services, inpatient hospital care, dental and ophthalmology programs, mobile clinics and other medical services."

Chapter Fourteen

Fields of Poison

Lettuce in all its varieties, cabbage, and cauliflower approached the heavy mid-summer harvest in the Salinas Valley, popularly called the "Salad Bowl of the World." Trucks transported hundreds of migrant farmhands to fields the morning of July 7, 1980. They descended on ranches to begin the backbreaking work of picking vegetables feeding one-third of America.

The same morning an employee of a pest control advisor notified a cauliflower rancher his fields required an application of pesticides. Two days later, July 9, the marketing cooperative to which the grower belonged informed the same advisor the harvest was slated for July 14. A pesticide applicator gave information to the cooperative it planned to spray pesticides the morning of July 10.

The grower and cooperative received all pesticide application data. The applicator filed a Notice of Intent with the California Agricultural Commissioner's office to spray fields with the highly toxic insecticides Phosdrin and Phosphamidon. The cooperative requested a harvesting crew go into the field the same day.

Unaccountably it received an affirmative response. The agent for the cooperative ordered the labor contractor to bring farmworkers to a cauliflower ranch on that date without informing him it had been sprayed with highly toxic insecticides. Shortly after midnight, July 10, Phosdrin and Phosphamidon were applied.

According to Section 2479c2(E) of the California Agricultural Code: *"Whenever a mixture of two or more organophosphate pesticides having a safety interval is applied, the safety interval shall be prolonged by adding to the longest applicable safety interval."*

Workers should have not been allowed to enter until seventy-two hours after the time of application. The code also requires *"Emergency medical care shall be planned for in advance. The employees or their supervisor in the field shall be informed of the name and location of a physician or medical facility that will provide emergency medical care... Fieldwork supervisors shall be informed of the usual symptoms of organophosphate and carbamate poisoning...When pesticide poisoning is suspected in an employee, the employer or his designated agent shall take the employee to a physician immediately."*

A low-lying mist flowed over vast fields of cauliflower, lettuce, and broccoli gleaming green under clouds that parted and closed over the sun. The subtle odor of garlic rose from the earth as fog came into contact with vegetation although garlic did not grow in the immediate vicinity (the odor is commensurate with moisture combining with organophosphates).

Men, women and children scrambled out of vehicles and headed into the field. They went to work without comment. Within minutes farm hands experienced severe burning in their eyes. They became disoriented and nauseous. Symptoms worsened and workers complained of acute physical problems.

The labor contractor suspected their extreme distress

158

was caused by pesticides. The marketing cooperative growing cauliflower assured the contractor workers could return to the field. The contractor drove to the pesticide applicator who briefed him that the area had been sprayed approximately six hours before fieldworkers arrived.

Returning to the ranch the contractor was horrified to find farm hands sprawled on the side of the field vomiting profusely. Two workers had extremely acute danger signs. One passed out. Another had difficulty standing or walking. The contractor drove them to the emergency room at Natividad Hospital.

The episode in 1964 when Antonio and his sister Meyo became violently ill after eating cherries flecked with a white substance immediately came to the forefront along with their father discounting his children's concern claiming that growers would have warned them of danger.

The rise of activism pushed for legislation to protect workers from aggravated poisoning situations. California Rural Legal Assistance team led by Bill Monning brought a pesticide poisoning case to the Division of Occupational Safety and Health (Cal/OSHA) in 1979. CRLA lost the initial hearing.

California Senator Bill Monning (billmonning.org)

One year later the major poisoning episode of July 10, 1980 broke out in Salinas. It had been eleven years after the Mondale hearing with Anthony Bianco Jr. Now farmworkers crowded emergency rooms at Natividad Medical Center and Salinas Valley Memorial Hospital.

Antonio rushed to the hospital and entered Dante's Inferno where a dozen men, women and children ranging in age from a nine-year old girl to a grandfather in his seventies staggered through the emergency room, sprawled on chairs and gurneys, threw up and screamed with pain. Doctors triaged patients and wheeled three suffering from extreme distress to Intensive Care.

"Physicians at Natividad quickly took their histories," recalled Antonio. "Patients were crying, had nasal discharge, nausea, diarrhea, vertigo, blurry vision coupled with slowing of the heartbeat. We called the Poison Control Center and Occupational Medical Clinic at the University of California San Francisco School of Medicine."

Physicians also contacted the County Agricultural Commissioner who checked permits for pesticide application. He reported that based on the crop (cauliflower) and the harvest date workers appeared to have been exposed to organophosphates.[82]

News of the incident traveled swiftly to Bill Monning at the Migrant Farm Worker Unit. He notified Natividad that his organization focused on impacts of pesticides on workers and rural residents. When Monning and his twenty-nine year old aide Juan Martínez arrived they promptly organized the Monterey County Pesticide Coalition (MCPC).

Molly Coye, M.D., MPH,[83] a medical investigative reporter for the Center of Disease Control (CDC) and Chief of the Occupational Health Clinic, San Francisco General Hospital, pulled together a team of toxicologists and epidemiologists to set up a laboratory at the newly formed pesticide coalition in Salinas to monitor patients.

Dr. Coye noted: "...there is no regular biologic monitoring of agriculture worker exposures to pesticides except for periodic cholinesterase tests required of certain pest control operators handling organophosphates and carbamate compounds on a regular basis in the state of California. There are no regular examinations or surveys to identify the adverse health effects of pesticide or pesticide residue exposure."[84]

Juan Martínez underscored the administrative aspects of the incident. Monning explored legal ramifications. Contacting workers who received no medical attention became their first task.

Natividad emergency room doctors confirmed a high probability that workers were exposed to an organophosphate or carbamate pesticide.[85] Carbamate is implicated in a variety of diseases including diabetes and cancer. Company doctors with privileges at Salinas Memorial Hospital claimed workers were not poisoned because their cholinesterase levels remained in the normal range. Their diagnoses proved incorrect over a ten to fifteen-week period. Depressed blood cholinesterase in farmworkers rising over fifty percent demonstrated clear evidence of poisoning.

The county hospital requested information from the National Institute of Occupational Safety and Health concerning organophosphate poisoning and consulted with a prominent toxicologist researching pesticides at the Berkeley Department of Public Health. Guided by data supplied by their sources Antonio and other physicians developed protocols for treating and assessing blood samples.

Agribusiness, chemical companies, and pesticide applicators cynically inferred that Natividad doctors, California Rural Legal Assistance, and United Farm Workers surreptitiously trained workers to mimic poisoning symptoms. In an attempt to play on racial stereotypes, they also claimed workers were hysterical or hung over from drinking.

Farmhands, many of whom were undocumented, resisted treatment due to concerns information would be passed to Immigration and Naturalization Services, even though Monning and Martínez promised they would

162

not reveal their status. It was only when workers learned that Antonio Velasco and Pablo Romero, M.D.[86] were Mexican-Americans who had worked in the fields that the majority of those impacted agreed to be tracked.

A few workers exposed to pesticides feared authorities would apprehend them and rejected medical services. To counter their fears Antonio gathered ambulatory farmworkers and made an impassioned plea that their lives and lives of co-workers depended on medical care.

"You have been poisoned with chemicals in the field. You should not have been taken there for at least forty-eight hours after they were sprayed," Antonio announced in Spanish. "Instead they drove you into the fields only six hours later. Your systems have been severely affected. If you return to the same farms or work next to a field that's been sprayed with pesticides you could die. We need information from your blood tests to determine what happened as a result of your exposure. No one has ever studied that. We have to understand what's going on before we permit you to return to work. Your bodies have been weakened. We need information from your blood tests to know how you are and if you can go back into the fields. We need you to stay home."

One of the workers stepped forward. His throat constricted as he talked. "*Si no trabajamos, no vamos a conseguir salario,*" he pleaded. ("If we don't work we will not be paid.") "We'll do our best to get you paid, but no promises," Antonio said.

Another farmworker stood on shaky legs. "We need to save our money," he said in English. "This is not right. We have been poisoned and now we'll lose money and maybe our jobs. We have to do something. You have to help us. You are a doctor, but you were once one of us. You have to help us find *abogados*, lawyers who know what to do."

"We're working with lawyers from California Rural Legal Assistance. They're going to fight for you. You can help yourselves by helping us. Lawyers need proof therefore we need to build a strong case to prevent this from happening to others in your family," insisted Antonio.

Farmworkers reacted emotionally on learning they had been placed in harm's way. They agreed to stay away from fields and cooperate with California Rural Legal Assistance by providing blood samples to doctors and scientists investigating the incident.

The Monterey County Pesticide Coalition followed twelve workers for fifteen weeks. Their cholinesterase levels regenerated at a meager half-a-percent a day. Medical literature indicated regeneration should register one percent a day.

In the midst of the 1980 crisis Charlie Clements who met Antonio at the AMSA conference in New Orleans and Julie Hurlocker arrived at Natividad to start their residency. Clements would eventually have a major impact on assessment and treatment of farm workers.

Physicians on staff at Salinas Memorial Hospital became dismayed when they discovered that several doctors under contract with agribusinesses, chemical companies, and pesticide operators acted against the best interest of poisoned farmworkers. Official records at the hospital indicated they hospitalized almost none of the impacted workers. Doctors under contract to the pesticide industry prescribed Atropine[87] to farm workers and informed them they could return to work.

"The medication gave a false sense of health improvement and well-being. It treats symptoms. If workers returned to the fields they could die," reported Antonio.

Clements had experience with Atropine in Vietnam. Pilots used the medication as an antidote against organophosphate nerve gases. U.S. aircraft dropped devices that sprayed an entire area paralyzing North Vietnamese troops. Rescue helicopters picking up downed pilots utilized Atropine to protect them from the worst effects of nerve gas.

"This was never publicized, of course, because it was a violation of international law to which the U.S. is a signatory. How nerve gas worked and how to be protected from it was something with which I was vaguely familiar. However during the incident in Salinas Molly Coye recommended using Protopam[88] as part of the protocol and it proved highly beneficial," stated Clements.

Natividad's ground-breaking diagnoses that pesticides presented a clear and present danger not only to workers, but also surrounding communities infuriated ranchers and farmers. The administration of the medical facility caved to threats of decreased funding while staff physicians refused to abandon patients and treated them on their own time. Their collective action forced Natividad to approve the establishment of a farmworker free clinic.

Patients who suffered from poisoning or thought they were poisoned became traumatized. "In a perverse way, it worked for us," recalled Antonio. "They didn't want to start work until they felt safe. We had time to monitor them every week. We provided care for which they were grateful. And we understood their pain and grief.

"Medical schools did not teach doctors how to talk with patients. They used the third person. They used a different tone of voice when talking to patients making them feel isolated."

CRLA held weekly community meetings giving workers progress reports concerning health care as well as legal remedies. The organization navigated, negotiated, and mediated internal squabbles with various factions of farmworker groups many of whom had family and ties to villages and towns in Mexico. A few patients demanded they return to work without a physician's clearance. Others entering the legal arena became anxious they might face deportation. The CRLA Migrant team and volunteers visited labor camps and homes to educate farmworkers about their rights under the law.

Existing protocols used by health care workers at the time required only a vague notion of a patient's work history. Women who came to Natividad had nothing in their charts about their occupation; what crops they harvested; or information about their employer in the event they gave birth to a severely handicapped child. The Salinas team upgraded protocol requirements and gathered detail information on each patient. With that data doctors could determine possible points of exposure.

Over the next twelve months two additional cases of mass poisonings occurred—three in one year. Antonio and Clements held press conferences using scientific evidence to bolster the fact that these were not isolated incidents. The Salinas Valley and every agricultural area of California presented a public health issue. Newspaper, television and radio coverage built momentum for a posting law with teeth warning workers of danger in the fields.

166

Clements immersed himself in the minutiae and data of farm worker issues in the Salinas Valley. His experience and research became the subject for his Master's in Public Health thesis, the backbone of legal and medical arguments utilized by CRLA and the scientific community. Statistics supplied sufficient information to file a case with Cal/OSHA on behalf of farmworkers. Plaintiffs had science on their side in the workers compensation case and in the later penalty phase.

The Natividad team originated the methodology that became an important tool in the public arena. "Every patient's blood test results followed the same slope. It led to the poisoning conclusion," remarked Antonio.

A month later CRLA reviewed a report from a physician paid by growers that was provided to the California Food and Drug Administration. The report stated: *"... their [workers'] cholinesterase[89] level was depressed but not to a level that would cause symptoms of organophosphate poisoning to develop. Many had complaints that indicated they knew the symptoms of organophosphate poisoning.... The patients he (a Natividad physician) saw could have returned to work."[90]*

Farm workers seen at Salinas Valley Memorial Hospital interacted with their compatriots treated at Natividad. They became indignant upon learning that the care provided at Salinas Valley Memorial was minimal and insufficient. Workers were told they could return to the fields in a few days. Doctors at Natividad warned them to stay away until the hospital received results of blood tests.

In an attempt to help workers overcome fears concerning activity in farm fields, Antonio and other doctors who had toiled as children and teenagers on farms throughout California accompanied farmhands to work.

"One worker who harvested lettuce had difficulty returning," recalled Antonio. "He broke into tremors and perspired profusely. We went into the fields with him. Because we had been in his shoes he trusted us. We tried to ease him back into work. He couldn't handle it and was so traumatized he returned to Mexico and never came back."

Chapter Fifteen

A Passion for Justice

Detailed, scientifically verified statistics and diagnoses of poisoning incidents from 1976 to 1980 became the foundation in documents issued by the Worker Health and Safety Unit, Division of Pest Management, Environmental Protection, and Worker Safety. The crux of announcements from the unit found that growers, chemical companies and pesticide applicators had primary responsibility for the incidents.

Four California counties providing the largest vegetable and fruit harvest to the United States and for export had the preponderance of illnesses due to exposure to organophosphates. In order of magnitude Monterey County had a total of fifty-four, followed by Kern County—thirty-one, Fresno County—twenty-six, and Imperial County–twenty-four. The majority occurred during the height of the July harvesting season.

A report regarding the Salinas Marketing Coop event stated: "Twenty-one field workers banding cauliflower before the 3-day reentry interval had expired were exposed to Mevinphos[91] and Phosphamidon residue... All workers were taken to hospital emergency rooms..."[92]

Legislators introduced pesticide bills in the 1981 California State Assembly session. The Salinas *Californian* reported "ten pesticide bills scheduled this week were postponed past the May 1 deadline for moving legislation through the policy committees of their house of origin.

"That means there will be no pesticide legislation emanating from the Assembly until 1983... [Richard] Lehman, D-Fresno and other farm area legislators were upset last January, when the board [State Water Resources Control Board] released a draft regulation for enforcing pesticide discharge limits from fields, and their collective pressure forced the board to back off."[93]

Agricultural communities in the San Joaquin, Salinas, and Central Valleys were by nature very conservative. Physicians who raised issues of farmworker safety risked endangering their practices.

"There is no reason doctors should not spend an hour on prevention as opposed to five minutes of treatment," Antonio Velasco insisted. "The difference is that the fee for treatment is fifty percent higher than a one-hour discussion about prevention."

Undeterred by the California Assembly's negative action not to enact pesticide legislation, CRLA brought the earlier 1979 pesticide poisoning case to the Cal/OSHA Appeals Board in 1981. Charlie Clements prepared a memorandum in the name of Natividad Medical Center that became a principal piece of evidence.

"The four physicians from CSVS (*Clínica de Salud del Valle de Salinas*) myself, Drs. Velasco, Romero, and O'Malley reviewed the physical and laboratory findings of the thirty two people that we examined... following the accidental exposure to phosdrin...it is not so much their acute condition as their susceptibility to any re-exposure with very vulnerable reserves of cholinesterase. Our recommendations are that the other

170

workers only return to work when the following conditions can be met: 1) the foreman of any crew that contains exposed workers should be informed of when and with what any field was sprayed which they are entering; 2) that the workers all wear appropriate protective clothing for the type of work they are doing; 3) that all exposed workers continue to have weekly monitoring of cholinesterase levels to insure that normal exposure to low residue does not prevent regeneration of enzymes."

A news report about the hearing stated in unambiguous terms: "The pest control advisor involved in Monterey County's worst known case of farmworker pesticide poisoning was compared to the My Lai massacre's Lt. William Calley Tuesday by a Salinas municipal court judge.

"Both may have served as fall guys for others equally involved indicated Judge Fred Novinger in imposing a minimal sentence upon Andy Alonzo of SoilServ.

"The 'others' in Alonzo's case may include the Monterey County agricultural commissioner and the rest of the county's agricultural community...An army lawyer during the Vietnam era, Novinger recalled being marginally involved in the investigations that ended with Calley being the only man to be sentenced for his part in the 1968 My Lai Massacre...

"Like Calley, Alonzo was a scapegoat, Novinger said. 'A guy at the bottom of the tube and a strong suspicion there are other people just as much involved'...

"The judge underscored that the laws Alonzo must obey include regulations linked to his pesticide advisory job.

"Novinger joined that to a pointed warning that he expected others in the agricultural community to do the same...'our community is in trouble...I tried to find some authority by which the local agricultural commissioner can waive, and I couldn't...I certainly hope our agricultural people are not taking it on themselves to just disregard the law'.

"Deputy District Attorney Robert Hatton...told the court he had no objection to the plea bargain that would exempt Alonzo from jail time...he still wanted some punishment...He suggested informal probation and a $300 fine.

"The D.A.'s recommended sentence and the sentence imposed by the court were denounced by Bill Monning of California Rural Legal Assistance, who is representing the twenty-two farmworkers before Cal/OSHA ... because the D.A. failed to go after others and the court was sympathetic to Alonzo's 'scapegoat' status 'the price for poisoning twenty-two farmworkers is $300. If that is the going rate, we can expect to see a lot more,' Monning said.

"Monning said his clients were still being medically monitored because of concerns that the intensity of their exposure to Phosdrin and Phosphamidon last July would render them more susceptible to other pesticides in the future." [94]

"It took synergy on a personal and activist level," said Antonio. "We stood on the shoulders of César Chávez and the United Farm Workers who organized field hands. Farmworker voices began to be heard gradually culminating as a formidable labor force."

Reporting on the 1981 poisoning incident, The Salinas *Californian* wrote: "Doctors at Natividad Medical Center have examined nine farmworkers who complained of exposure on Sunday to herbicides applied to a field off Hitchcock Road.

"A crew foreman took one of the unidentified workers, who suffered severe nausea and vomiting, to Salinas Valley Memorial Hospital shortly after the workers entered the field at 6 a.m. Hospital spokesmen said the man was treated and later released.

"Information gathered by investigators for the Monterey County Agricultural Commissioner's Office indicates that the crew was laying irrigation pipe on the perimeter of a newly planted field of cauliflower.

"The herbicides Dacthal and Vegedex had been applied fourteen hours earlier and had dried.

"'As far as we're concerned, there have been no violations of rules governing use of the chemicals, Chick Legault, assistant agricultural commissioner, said today.

"The field is part of the Bardin Ranch and farmed by California Coastal Farms. Cal Coastal President Walter Bryggman and company attorneys declined to comment on the incident.

"Blood tests performed on the worker who suffered the worst side effects showed a 'significant' level of exposure, but the man returned to work the following day, said Dr. Antonio Velasco at Natividad.

"Velasco said he and Dr. Michael O'Malley took blood samples from the other eight on Tuesday and found little evidence that they had been poisoned.

"However, he said, all eight complained of headaches and mild nausea.

"Legault said his office investigated only the one complaint so far because he has not yet received doctors' reports on the other eight workers... Growers are not currently required to post fields that have been sprayed...[95]"

Word of *Coalición de Salud del Valle* quickly spread throughout the migrant worker community. Agitated farm hands distressed about pesticide poisoning incidents flocked to the free clinic in Salinas. Among them were Salvadorans who escaped the civil war in their homeland.

Charlie Clements listened to disturbing, horrific tales of murder, rape, and torture endured by Salvadoran migrants in their home country. Their firsthand report of thousands of union members, clergy, independent farmers, students and university officials executed impacted his moral conscience. The tipping point came when a woman who worked on local farms told him a death squad in El Salvador murdered her schoolteacher daughter.

Clements refused to stand by while innocent civilians came under siege. He took a leave from Natividad and traveled to El Salvador to transport medical supplies on his back to thousands of civilians. He escaped bombs, rockets and strafing while carrying out his humanitarian mission.

Although the Natividad team missed Charlie Clements' presence, they understood and admired his altruistic motive to enter a raging civil war. The conflict in El Salvador proved problematic when it was disclosed that the United States secretly funded a right-wing militia to fight the popular left-wing Farabundo Martí National Liberation Front (FMLN). The U.S. supported militia massacred over 800 civilians half of whom were children. It assassinated Monsignor Oscar Romero the liberal Archbishop of San Salvador. The Vatican canonized the Archbishop in 2018.

Another battle to save lives took place in Monterey County. Hearings were held to post signs in Spanish and

English warning farm workers to stand clear of farms sprayed with pesticides.

"It was clear there was no way workers, or the general public could know when the fields were treated with dangerous pesticides, therefore no way to prevent poisonings. Signs warning people were required when and wherever chemicals had been applied. Workers had to wait a required time before it was safe to enter," reported Antonio.

"By this time we had won a big settlement for the initial mass poisoning and were positioned strongly with our peer-reviewed publications and our approved protocol for diagnosis and management of organophosphates. Additionally, we had gathered support from CRLA leadership, San Francisco Occupational Medicine Department, California Public Health Department, and the community of Monterey County.

"We had one supportive member of the County Board of Supervisors. But, above all, it was a logical next step in our work to continue on the public health approach. Bill Monning and Charlie Clements before he departed for El Salvador felt strongly we could win this fight and prevent individuals from becoming victims of poisonings. I felt the same way," said Antonio.

He outlined the rationale for demanding warning posters in fields. "Pushing for the posting regulation would only bring us better publicity and public support, especially when we appealed to the larger community so it wouldn't be viewed as a 'farmworker' issue only.

"Salinas is surrounded by fields and there are schools right next to them. It became an issue that affected everyone in the county. As a result, the Pesticide Coalition was formed by a very diverse group of people, many of whom were voters and active in politics. The board of supervisors could not ignore these people. The only downside was the persistent personal attacks on some of us from the growers and pesticide applicators.

"But our perseverance and legal victories, with large awards and fines for growers and applicators, eventually made them realize it was actually to their benefit. If they posted fields and contractors took a crew in any way they would no longer be liable, the contractor would.

"At the state level we had the support of people like State Director for CRLA Ralph Lightstone; Molly Coye director of the UCSF occupational medicine clinic; and many other friends of Bill Monning.

"Our opposition was the same as in the beginning, from growers and applicators. By this time they were losing support in the community and seen for what they were: people interested in profits regardless of health consequences. Also, because of documented medical proof we were no longer written off as 'anti pesticide activists' who only exaggerated the magnitude of the problem for political reasons."

The hearings resulted in Richard Nutter, the county agricultural commissioner, issuing emergency regulations on field worker safety. It stated: *"No person shall apply any pesticide for which there is an established safety interval of twenty-four hours or longer unless the area to be treated has been posted..."*[96]

The San Jose Mercury reported "Signs warning that lettuce fields have been sprayed with deadly pesticides went up Monday [June 15, 1981] around Monterey County, where officials hope they will help save workers from unnecessary exposure to toxic substances.

"The county ordinance, the only one of its kind in California, came after two incidents in the last 11 months in which fifty-eight field workers were exposed to pesticides because they entered the fields too soon after spraying.

"The regulation requires signs to bear a skull and crossbones and to be marked 'Danger—Do Not Enter' in both English and Spanish. Violation of the ordinance, which also prohibits growers from ordering workers into fields where signs are posted, brings a maximum $500 fine and six months in jail."[97]

Emergency regulations were revised in 1983 to permanent posting regulations with a provision that *"any person who violates any provision of this regulation is subject to civil and criminal penalties set for in the Food and Agricultural Sections 11891 through 11894."*

An article in the Monterey County Weekly in 2003 quoted Bill Monning: "The growers and applicators did not like the idea of skulls and crossbones on the edge of fields for tourists and consumers to see. Nor did the agricultural industry want to pay the extra costs associated with posting."[98]

Antonio's energy and devotion to a life-saving cause impressed Monning. "We don't all start at the same place. We don't all encounter the obstacles, barriers, deterrents that he overcame. Antonio has a burning passion for justice. He converted his anger into achievement."

After the successful outcome in Monterey Antonio Velasco took a leave of absence from Natividad and his practice. He toured the western states presenting findings of the Salinas team of doctors and scientists on the dangers of pesticides to field workers, farm worker advocates, and growers.

During his whirlwind circuit he received a call from Bill Monning informing him that the Subcommittee on Department Operations, Research, and Foreign Agriculture of the Committee on Agriculture, House of Representatives planned to hold FIFRA hearings in Washington, D.C. on June 16, July 16, and 22, 1981. Cal/OSHA, Rural Legal Assistance Fund, and United Farm Workers requested Antonio's permission to place him on the Thursday, July 16, 1981 agenda to provide expert testimony just as he had done in Monterey.

FIFRA, Federal Insecticide, Fungicide, and Rodenticide Act had its origins during the enlightened administration of President William Howard Taft who expanded Theodore Roosevelt's battle against monopolies and succeeded in breaking the stranglehold over business by forcing Standard Oil and the American Tobacco Company to sell their subsidiaries to independent operators thus opening competition in the marketplace.

Cognizant that farmers were small business owners who required protection against harmful insecticides and ordinary citizens who needed to feel secure that the produce they ate would not harm them, Taft bucked the manufacturers of pesticides who claimed their products were not harmful and signed into law the Federal Insecticide Act of 1910.

The act did little to protect the environment or public health, but it took a first step in regulating the use of poisons in the environment. In the ensuing years chemical companies prospered by developing new and more powerful pesticides that warring factions during World War One transformed into poison gas. Nazi Germany converted a cyanide-based pesticide into Zyklon B the preferred agent to kill innocent men, women and children forced into gas chambers during World War Two.

178

FIFRA addressed pesticide concerns in 1947. The act has been amended several times to tighten regulations protecting both farmers and consumers although enforcement of the law has been irregular depending on government funding of the Environmental Protection Agency.

Chapter Sixteen

Denial of Reality

Powerful representatives from the National Agricultural Chemicals Association (NACA), the Pesticide Producers Association, and pesticide distributors packed a meeting room in the impressive Neo-classic Revival Longworth Building on Independence Avenue south of the Capital Mall for the first hearing on June 16, 1981.

The presiding member of the committee, Representative George E. Brown, Jr., Democrat from California opened the session with a statement of purpose.

"Our major focus during this session will be on issues related to the handling and treatment of safety, health and environmental effects data submitted by pesticide companies to the Environmental Protection Agency in support of an application for registration.

"[Congress has] stood firm behind the principle that the public should have access to safety and health data [while] the pesticide industry raises legitimate concerns about the potential sacrifice of market advantages if competitors also have ready access to valuable data...

"...I am confident that real solutions and workable compromises can be found... I shall proceed undaunted and optimistic and best yet, without further distractions and with

180

the minimum of further intervention on my part..."[99]

The pesticide industry argument centered primarily on the financial burden companies would carry under more restrictive regulations. They also objected to revealing chemical formulas out of concern that the revelation would diminish competitive advantage.

Jack D. Early, President of the National Agricultural Chemical Association summed up their self-serving objections: "NACA is particularly concerned about the harm of disclosure to entities which seek registration on an international basis in other countries. If data are not adequately protected, U. S. technology could be misappropriated either domestically or internationally...NACA's proposals [do not] infringe upon the public's right to know the scientific basis for decisions by EPA on pesticide registrations and the effect of chemicals in the environment. The proposals involve the protection of competitively valuable research and test data, developed at enormous risk and expense..."[100]

The Pesticide Producers Association's written testimony revealed their underlying interest regarding legitimate, factual scientific data: "...the industry has no problem with supplying this data nor with providing information when actually required for the purpose of supporting the continued registration of pesticide products. It does not feel that it is necessary to provide data on the basis of a scientific witch hunt..."

The president of the Chemical Specialties Manufacturers Association, Ralph Engel, suggested narrowing the scope of regulation including rules that require appropriate labeling of pesticides that inform consumers about the variety of chemicals in products.

"There is misunderstanding and inconsistency with respect to labeling requirements generally caused by the use of EPA handouts which either recommend or require a format contrary to existing labeling regulations...These procedures confuse the industry which is trying to comply with existing regulations..."

Every industry association concentrated on the financial burden placed upon the shoulders of their members. They considered almost all regulations to inform the public about the formulation of products onerous and overwhelming. They emphasized profit over public health by avoiding any discussion in connection with the impact of pesticides on men, women, and children.

Attitudes had not radically changed since the 1969 hearings chaired by Senator Walter Mondale when a grape grower responded to the senator's question about contaminated grapes with a surprising answer: "Why would I take a bunch of grapes from a store to a laboratory?"

Farmworkers became ill, endured neurologic damage, and female workers suffered miscarriages. Workers appeared as expendable as they were when Pauline Kibbe, Executive Secretary of the Good Neighbor Commission of Texas wrote in 1956: "Generally speaking, the Latin-American migratory worker going into west Texas is regarded as a necessary evil, nothing more nor less than an unavoidable adjunct to the harvest season. Judging by the treatment that has been accorded him in that section of the state, one might assume that he is not a human being at all, but a species of farm implement that comes mysteriously and spontaneously into being."[101]

Environmental groups coalesced to counter industry

claims they were treated unfairly. Jacqueline M. Warren, National Resources Defense Council, an organization primarily involved in safeguarding the earth, its people, its plants and animals, and the natural systems on which all life depends, stated in part: "It is patently unfair to exclude members of the public from challenging the adequacy of pesticide regulatory decisions in hearings for the Agency, while guaranteeing the right of the pesticide user and user groups to challenge the stringency of such decisions."

Ms. Warren summarized the views of the National Resources Defense Council with a forceful reminder that "... amendments to FIFRA were enacted following extensive debate and a herculean effort to accommodate the interests of all concerned. The issues resolved by those amendments should not be re-debated absent compelling evidence that the remedies adopted have not been successful..."[102]

The National Audubon Society's Policy Analyst Maureen K. Hinkle had been the pesticides monitor for the Audubon Society and the Environmental Defense Fund for seven years during which time she observed EPA's implementation of FIFRA. She outlined the dangers unregulated pesticides had on the future. "Their use will expand even more dramatically in the next decades. The Global 2000 Study, released by the CEQ [Council on Environmental Quality] and the State Department in July 1980 projected that pesticides and fertilizers will double in the developed countries and quadruple for the developing countries by the year 2000... If regulation of pesticides fails to get a handle on use there will be more dramatic problems demanding attention...

"As one federal official put it, 'It's a mine field out there and we don't know where (or when) the next one will go off.'

Regulation of pesticides must address expanding production, sales, and use."[103]

The EPA and members of the committee sent requests for information from chemical companies. Almost all corporate entities refused to disclose any data with respect to "specific active ingredients" in their pesticide formulas. Rep. Brown brought the hearing to a close and announced the next date would be July 16.

The temperature in Washington, D.C. on July 15, 1981 hovered near eighty degrees with eighty-one percent humidity. It had the effect of making it feel close to a damp ninety degrees. The air-conditioned hotel room gave Antonio respite from the heat. Before reviewing his notes for the meeting on the following day he phoned Isabel. She wished him good luck at the hearing. Salinas' weather was a comfortable eighty degrees with a cool breeze blowing in from the ocean. Antonio responded that the only thing blowing in from Chesapeake Bay were swarms of mosquitoes.

The next morning he walked from the hotel to the nearby Longworth Building. In the normally staid, button-down nation's capital jackets came off and ties loosened. Women wore lightweight blouses, dresses, skirts and slacks.

Inside the cool environs of the meeting room Antonio Velasco, Robert C. Spear, Professor of Environmental Health Sciences, School of Public Health, University of California, Berkeley, and Paula DiPerna, a writer and journalist based in New York, sat at a baize-covered table before the committee.

Representative George E. Brown, Jr. gaveled the room to order promptly at 9:45 a.m. "I want to welcome those in attendance this morning...Today our purpose is to hear testimony on whether and to what extent our pesticide

184

law is protecting public safety and health from negligent or illegal use of pesticides. No one benefits from pesticide misuse. When a company's product causes a human health problem from misuse, the public's confidence in what may be a perfectly safe and efficacious product may be compromised if not shattered... Our guiding principle in this endeavor is simply and widely shared. The public's health should not be needlessly jeopardized by a pesticide applicator's carelessness, by a lack of respect for the law, or by an unwillingness or inability to enforce the law.

"This afternoon we will also hear testimony from agricultural and chemical representatives on safety and health issues...We will begin this morning with a panel of three witnesses...Our first witness is Dr. Antonio Velasco who is an M.D. from Natividad Hospital in Salinas, California.

"We welcome him not only because of his expertise but also because he is from California and is much better qualified to speak on this subject...."[104]

Although he didn't require a prepared statement Antonio carefully unfolded his notes on the green felt to insure he covered all his points.

"I am a doctor at the Natividad Medical Center which is the county hospital of Monterey located in Salinas, California. The Natividad Medical Center provides primary and emergency care for the indigent population of the county. "The majority of my patients are farmworkers. For the past two years I have worked in all the wards of the hospital including the family practice clinic, the obstetrics ward, and the emergency rooms.

"I am also the medical director of the recently established farmworker clinic, *La Clínica Popular*, also located

185

in Salinas. The farmworker clinic has developed a program designed to respond to the incidents of pesticide poisonings in the Salinas Valley.

"There exists a serious problem of pesticide-related illnesses in the Salinas Valley. The number of reported pesticide-related illnesses has doubled in Monterey County since 1979. The statistics available do not reflect unreported pesticide exposures or poisonings for a variety of reasons.

"In my work I have treated numerous pesticide related illnesses including three mass poisonings of farmworkers within the last year. I have dealt with both the acute and chronic effects of pesticide exposure and would like to thank this committee for the opportunity to detail some of those experiences for you today.

"Last July I was called upon to treat nineteen field workers who were acutely poisoned after they were taken into a field sprayed with two highly toxic organophosphates, Phosdrin and Phosphamidon. In this case the workers exposed ranged in age from a nine-year-old girl to a 72-year-old man. The workers had been tying cauliflower, a procedure that requires the placement of a rubber band around the leaves of the cauliflower plant prior to harvesting.

"When Phosdrin and Phosphamidon are used together as insecticides there exists a 72-hour reentry period. No worker is to enter a field for a minimum of 72 hours after the application of these chemicals. The workers I treated had been taken to the field approximately five hours after the chemicals were applied. As such, we cannot adequately assess the full extent of the medical effects of this particular exposure.

"On April 23 of this year I was once again called upon

to respond to a mass poisoning of farmworkers. In this case, thirty-eight workers and three agricultural inspectors were exposed to the organophosphate Phosdrin just hours after it had been applied in a lettuce field. Once again workers were taken into the field before the re-entry period had expired. We are still treating twenty-eight of the workers who were poisoned in this incident. The symptoms manifested in this care are similar to those described in the first poisoning case.

"In addition to these two cases I recently treated a worker who was exposed to pesticide drift [105] because of an aerial application in a field adjacent to where our patient worked. In general we have seen a steady influx of workers exposed to pesticides at the job site.

"We have become increasingly aware of patients manifesting symptoms suggestive of pesticide poisoning. For many of the patients treated we identified pesticide residues in the patient's blood through the use of gas chromatography, a procedure that enables us to detect even minute quantities of pesticide residues.

"Although this procedure is helpful to identify the presence of certain toxins in the patient's blood, there is a general lack of information that shows the direct cause and effect of various chemical agents.

"In the two mass poisoning cases where we treated patients there were apparent problems in the application procedure, which, if averted, could have prevented the incidents from taking place:

"One, the re-entry periods were not observed and consequently workers were exposed prematurely to highly toxic insecticides;

"Two, no signs were posted indicating the presence of

toxic chemical, re-entry times, or the names of the chemicals used;

"Three, industry procedures following the poisonings made it difficult for us to ascertain the names of chemicals used in the fields;

"Four, industry procedures made it difficult for us to guarantee the safety of the workers following the acute exposures because the employers recalled workers prior to medical clearance;

"Five, the fact that no red blood cell base lines exist for farmworkers makes it difficult to assess the severity of organophosphate poisoning cases.

"In addition to the acute effects of the poisonings mentioned, we are becoming increasingly concerned about the potential carcinogenic, mutagenic, and teratogenic effects of many chemicals currently in use.

"In Monterey County the neo-natal death rate for the Spanish surnamed population is double that of the non-Spanish population.

"In Imperial County, an agricultural region in Southern California with many of the same crops which are in production in Monterey County, a recent study reflects a birth defect rate among farmworker women that is 300% greater than the national norm.

"The rate of anencephalics, babies born with an undeveloped brain, is disproportionally high in Monterey County. I have detected the presence of pesticide poisoning in pregnant patients.

"Unfortunately, I have no access to adequate medical data on the potential effects of pesticide exposure to various chemicals during pregnancy.

188

"My efforts to obtain such data have been fruitless despite many calls to medical experts and health agencies, including the EPA's National Poison Control Center. As such, I have no means by which to gauge the potential for birth defects or abnormal fetal development because of exposure to various chemicals. Further, developmental disorders in children are difficult, if not impossible to correlate with prenatal exposure to various chemicals.

"Many of the patients treated for exposure to organophosphates have displayed symptoms of impaired memory and memory disorder. We do not know the long term or chronic nature of this disorder, particularly among children who were exposed.

"I have attempted to obtain data on health effects for various chemical agents through a number of efforts. I contacted the Environmental Protection Agency's Poison Control Center for health data on certain chemicals but have been unable to obtain satisfactory results.

"I also utilized a computer search system of the University of California's data on toxic substances and pesticides but have been unsuccessful in acquiring the needed data.

"I have contacted other agencies and medical centers but have been frustrated in my efforts to acquire information that would assist me in the diagnosis and treatment of many patients.

"I have been overwhelmed by calls from members of the general public who have expressed concerns about exposure to pesticides because of drift into residential areas.

"The current spraying of Malathion in Santa Clara County has prompted inquiries regarding the potential effects of organophosphate exposure to pregnant women and others.

"In general, the agricultural industry and the administrative agencies in Monterey County have been insensitive to the problem faced by the medical community. I can only describe the seriousness of pesticide exposures in Monterey County as vast in proportion.

"There is insufficient training of health personnel both in medical schools and in rural communities with respect to diagnosis and treatment of pesticide cases. In my opinion there has been insufficient enforcement of pesticide regulations leading to the increased exposure of workers to pesticides.

"As a doctor in an agricultural area I can only describe the seriousness of pesticide exposure in Monterey County as epidemic in nature.

"I have experienced first-hand the seriousness of pesticide exposures both in terms of the effects of such poisonings on the patients and the demands placed upon the hospital to respond both logistically to mass poisonings and adequately to patients who we know have been exposed or are continuing to be exposed to chemicals for which we have little if any medical data related to chronic effects.

"As a medical professional, I hope that this committee will take action to increase the protection to workers and others living in rural areas from unnecessary exposures to pesticides.

"I would also hope that action taken by this committee will lead to the establishment of regulations which will provide treating doctors with all pertinent medical data which may be available to manufacturers or others so that we can provide quality diagnosis and treatment to victims of pesticide poisoning."[106]

Dr. Robert Spear summarized his findings: "I would

190

like to point out that we have very little idea of the real nature and extent of the adverse impact of chemicals on agricultural workers. Even in California where we have a reasonable reporting system all we are likely to turn up are acute problems and often not even those among undocumented workers.

"In the long haul any rational regulatory program requires the collection of data on the health status of the population being protected for evaluation and for planning.

"In agriculture even the worksite moves, and traditional epidemiological approaches are very difficult to apply, and few have tried to overcome these inherent difficulties.

"Nonetheless, the time has come to send epidemiologists into the field, the vineyard, and orchard. If a clear mandate is given through FIFRA to deal comprehensively with worker safety and health, this issue can, at least, be raised to a position of visibility and, in some favorable fiscal future, we may begin to learn something of the health status of our agricultural work force."[107]

The committee opened for questions to the panel. Representative Brown directed his first query to Antonio Velasco.

"Can you give us some estimate as to the familiarity of other physicians in your county and other parts of California with regard to this problem and their level of awareness about the nature of the problem?"

Antonio responded: "...a lot of physicians are not only unaware that there is a legal requirement to report the pesticide related illnesses, but there is a general lack of knowledge about the diagnosis and treatment because...there is very little training in medical school...awareness is low and minimal both in the county where I work and in the State in general."

Rep. Brown followed up with a specific question: "What kind of system could you suggest that might allow us to fill the data gaps or disseminate more adequately the data we have?"

Antonio recommended "...if I could have direct access either through a local call or at the very least through a call to a nearby poison control center that would have available data that is most recent on the chemicals.

"For example, I have a patient suffering from pesticide symptoms. She was five months pregnant...I documented that she had levels in her blood of a very toxic chemical, thiodan. In spite of my efforts to get information on that from the Environmental Protection Agency and local and State experts, I was not able get any of it...with some of these chemicals I have a suspicion that there is a lot more known than I have access to as a medical professional...

"...I am concerned if there is any information available or that is found during the research to show that chemicals are either safe or not safe, that information should be made available to physicians.

"Otherwise we are really unable to advise our patients adequately in terms of what risks they have, if any, or to reassure them there are no risks..."[108]

David Pechan, a former crop dusting pilot from Mendocino, California testified that he "...quit approximately two years ago. I became disgusted with the lack of enforcement by the EPA or the FAA. In fact in my four years in California I was never visited by the FAA at all."[109]

The avalanche of criticism against the lack of toxic chemical enforcement became more prominent as university law professors, and representatives of the Migrant Legal

Assistance Program and California Rural Legal Assistance bolstered Antonio Velasco's statement.

An organized rebuttal countered the facts presented by Antonio and others regarding the necessity to open data on research, formulation, and adverse reactions to the millions of pounds of pesticides poured on farms growing agricultural products.

Chemical associations, representatives of corporate agribusiness, chemical applicators, and scientists with research funded by chemical companies denied workers had been affected by pesticide poisoning.

Jack D. Early, President of the National Agricultural Chemicals Association who testified in the June hearing appeared before the committee and admitted proudly "The member companies of NACA produce virtually all the pesticides used in the United States for agricultural purposes — both the basic pest control chemicals and the end-use pesticides formulated from these basic chemicals."[110]

In an attempt to divert attention away from domestic regulation, Early pointed to regulations requiring proper labeling for products imported to the United States. He also quoted from EPA regulations requiring manufacturers who export pesticides to notify foreign governments that a pre-shipment statement "serves the purpose of alerting the foreign government that a certain pesticide is entering its country."

Early concluded his testimony with a conspicuous corporate statement that ignored notification of pesticide dangers in the domestic market: "...these issues are important to both the EPA and the industry. Export notification is necessary to advise other countries about chemicals which are being shipped internationally but procedures must not impose unreasonable burdens upon industry."[111]

The successful work accomplished by Antonio and his team came under attack from Steve Keil, Chairman of the Farm Chemicals Committee, National Association of Wheat Growers.

"The situation that has evolved in California is a disaster for the California Department of Food and Agriculture, for the registrant of pesticide products, and ultimately for California agriculture...Approval of pesticide usage and establishment of pesticide tolerances is an area where international cooperation is desirable to avoid artificial trade barriers. *Individual state activity* [emphasis added] in this field is wasteful and chaotic."[112]

Pesticide advocates placed "trade secrets" above the health and welfare of the American public. One of the concluding documents submitted to the committee brought the issue back to the dangers of pesticides.

Anthony Trujillo worked as an applicator for three Salinas Valley chemical companies. In sworn deposition he reported: "While working for Oxy Chem I was involved in an incident which reflects the lack of concern for human health and the lack of enforcement of sanctions for violations. An applicator with the company had applied insecticides to an artichoke field in Castroville. After he had finished the application which was adjacent to a residential area he had a surplus of chemical in his tanks and proceeded to dump about 150-200 gallons of insecticide in a hole which had been dug by children in a play area...[after it was reported] We proceeded to pour fresh dirt over the chemical using a tractor scoop but the chemical itself was not removed and the area was still accessible for children to play. No fine or other disciplinary action was initiated to my knowledge."[113]

Ralph Lightstone, California Rural Legal Assistance, presented amendments requiring the EPA administrator to issue regulations providing for the safe use of pesticides. He also presented factual data that manufacturing groups "pointed to the current California registration data requirements as the problem... "[114]

He further stated: "...NACA and CSMA (The National Agricultural Chemical Association and Chemical Specialty Manufacturers Association) along with fifteen pesticide companies, sued the State of California seeking to enjoin its registration regulations on a theory of federal preemption."[115]

The Federal Court denied the motion and dismissed the challenge. However in April 1980 under pressure from industry California amended its data requirements.

Industry groups were not satisfied and sponsored a bill to repeal all new registration regulations. They misjudged California's determination to be a leader in pesticide reform.

Lightstone reported "The bill was defeated largely because grower groups, farmworker groups, and environmentalists had all reached agreement on the acceptability of the revised regulations."[116]

A massive lobbying campaign by chemical companies, agribusiness corporations, and pesticide applicators halted Federal legislation requiring adequate data for researchers and physicians to diagnose patients suffering from pesticide poisoning and the simple action of placing warning posters on all farms—similar to legislation in California. Threatened by major donors from those organizations representatives and senators on both sides of the aisle quashed legislation to protect farm worker health.

The Monterey County regulations were adopted throughout the State of California. Two years later in 1983 Representative Tom Harkin, Democrat from Iowa and Senator William Proxmire, Democrat from Wisconsin introduced the same issues in the 98th U.S. Congress. They wrote the National Pesticide Hazard Protection Act (NPHPA). The measure had support from health, farm, consumer, and environmental organizations.

Staff reductions in the Environmental Protection Agency under the Reagan administration wreaked havoc with upholding environmental standards. FIFRA (Federal Insecticide, Fungicide, and Rodenticide Act) required reauthorization in 1983. Members of congress side-stepped pesticide issues while reform advocates requested at least a one-year extension of the law to introduce reforms and a national review of protocols to protect the public from pesticide exposure.

Representative Leon Panetta,[117] Democrat from California, and Representative Steve Gunderson, Republican from Wisconsin allegedly influenced by corporate farming interests in their states issued a statement that they did not think "it is appropriate to take on any such controversial issues during an election year."[118]

Subsequently the House passed a one-year extension of the law. Panetta and Gunderson introduced a two-year extension on the National Pesticide Hazard Protection Act

196

reiterating they wished to avoid any debate during the election.

As time progressed other counties in California as well as states adopted Monterey County regulations formulated by Antonio Velasco and the Salinas team bypassing the crushing dominance of corporate interests over the health and welfare of the American public.

The positive outcome achieved in Monterey coincided with good news. Isabel became pregnant with her second child in January 1982. The fact that poisoning incidents did not cease in the Salinas Valley could not dampen the parents' happiness although the chemical industry kept up a ruthless, unrelenting attack on Antonio's character.

Salinas *Californian* reporter Paul Engstrom wrote a follow-up story to his original piece that Agricultural Labor Relations workers were exposed to pesticides.

"Two people remained hospitalized today after they were apparently exposed to a combination of pesticides Friday morning outside the Agricultural Labor Relations Board office on Boronda Road, officials said.

"Dr. Antonio Velasco, one of several physicians participating in Natividad's farm worker clinic said [the employee an ALRB attorney] suffered moderate and mild exposure to a combination of three pesticides...

"Authorities suspect the chemicals were Lannate, an insecticide considered hazardous for at least twenty-four hours after application; Meta-Systox R, an insecticide with a forty-eight-hour field re-entry period; and Dithane M22, a fungicide with no re-entry limit...

"Verticare[119] was spraying the Quattrin Ranch field... But Jim Cheatham, president of Verticare, said this morning

197

he had not been contacted about the incident…He doubted the seriousness of reported illnesses, if they were caused by the chemicals dropped by Verticare."[120]

The Salinas *Californian* continued to investigate the situation with a story that reported: "Tests on an Agricultural Labor Relations Board field agent indicated a below normal red-blood cell count…Antonio Velasco, a doctor at Natividad's farmworker clinic confirmed the findings but declined to discuss them. Velasco forwarded his results on Monday to Walter Wong, County Director of Environmental Health.

"Jim Cheatham, President of Verticare, which applied the chemical to a field off Ramona Road, said Tuesday that he suspects the ALRB worker and Dr. Velasco exaggerated the spray incident in an effort to generate bad publicity for pesticide applicators. 'Everything I've looked at indicates we have a political situation going on here,' said Cheatham characterizing the affair as a conspiracy launched by anti-pesticide advocates.

"But Lupe Martínez, director of the ALRB regional office here, rejected the charge saying: 'Mr. Cheatham is just wrong'… Noting that his employees were in the parking lot at the time, not in the target field to south, Martínez added 'There is no plan to get anyone… The county Health Department has finished interviewing the ALRB employees and their co-workers Wong said this morning. But Wong said he won't forward his findings to county Agricultural Commissioner Richard Nutter and the state Department of Health until Nutter has completed a parallel investigation.

"A state laboratory in Sacramento is examining samples taken from foliage and windshields of cars parked near the ALRB office Friday. The cauliflower field sprayed by Verticare is about 100 yards south of the office."[121]

Disturbed by insensitive treatment of farm workers a cadre of doctors from Salinas Memorial Hospital informed Antonio that one of the medical chiefs at their hospital complained that Natividad physicians were incompetent. The unfounded charge incentivized Antonio's team to double down on their research and permit facts to speak for them rather than engage in a verbal brawl with opposing physicians.

The chemical industry continued its assault on Antonio Velasco despite the successful adoption of regulations in Monterey County for warning postings. James Cheatham picked up the charge of incompetency on behalf of pesticide manufacturers and applicators. He petitioned the Monterey County Board of Supervisors requesting an investigation of the physician.

"I understand that Antonio Velasco is a Monterey County employee working for the Natividad Medical Center. Dr. Velasco receives a lot of news media attention for claims of pesticide poisoning. Many of these claims are considered very questionable by people who are competent in this field. He has contradicted other medical doctors by hospitalizing people who were released by the other doctor [sic]. Other, very experienced and knowledgeable authorities on the subject of pesticide poisoning do not receive the media attention he does.

"My company, VERTICARE, has recently been implicated in the press, by what we think may be a flagrant example of misdiagnosis. Our concern is based on the fact that conclusions drawn by Dr. Velasco differ so greatly from our own very considerable experience and knowledge of pesticide exposure. After all, we are the people who handle the materials in undiluted form on a daily basis, and we don't experience problems such as he describes from what could at most be only a tiny exposure compared to ours.

"My concern is over the possibility that Dr. Velasco, in his zeal as an anti-pesticide activist, may be letting his politics overrule his medicine. If this results in his making a false or incorrect diagnosis, then it could seriously threaten the health of his patients and would be the very worst kind of malpractice.

"I would like to go on record for an investigation of Dr. Velasco's record in diagnosing pesticide poisoning. I trust this could be carried out by broadly recognized experts on the subject.

"If I can be of any help to you with sources of information or additional facts, please don't hesitate to call. Thank you for your kind consideration."[122]

One day later on July 23, 1982 E. R. Marshall President of Soilserv, Inc. a provider of wholesale agricultural chemicals joined the growing ranks of those opposed to Antonio in another letter to the Monterey County Board of Supervisors.

"I have been advised that Mr. James R. Cheatham, by a letter to Mr. Marc Del Piero has filed a request with the Monterey County Board of Supervisors for an investigation of Dr. Antonio Velasco's record in diagnosing and treatment of patients who he claims have been overexposed to pesticides.

"Soilserv has had similar experiences with Dr. Velasco and his diagnosis and treatment, which is often in contradiction to diagnosis' [sic] of other doctors who are recognized experts in the field.

"We fully support Mr. Cheatham's request and would welcome the opportunity to discuss our experiences with a qualified investigation team.

"We are concerned about the health and safety of the farmers of Monterey County. Pesticides must be applied to protect the crops vital to the welfare of all in the County.

"Scare raising and publicity tactics as used by Dr. Velasco do nothing for the citizens of this County.

"We believe a thorough investigation of his practices are [sic] warranted."[123]

In an attempt to garner public support for the investigation Cheatham wrote an opinion piece published in the Salinas *Californian* on August 12, 1982 outlining his view on the subject of pesticide poisoning.

"Since Paul Engstrom failed to report facts I gave him, concerning the alleged spray incident involving Agricultural Labor Relations Board Staff members, I would like to pass the following information on to the public:

"1. There was a man washing his van on the property between ALRB (Agricultural Labor Relations Board) and the field being sprayed. He states he was not sprayed, suffered no ill effects, and that the wind was blowing in the wrong direction to have drifted on the ALRB property.

"2. Dithane M-22 is a yellow wettable powder, which leaves a visible residue where it is deposited. The Agricultural Commissioner's inspectors found no visible spots whatsoever on the ALRB property.

"3. Lannate SP is highly toxic only in the oral mode. This means you would have to drink it in order for it to be highly toxic. It is not readily absorbed through the skin.

"4. Metasystox R is only a class 2 pesticide. This means you can buy it at Long's Drugs, and use it on your shrubbery at home without ill effects.

"5. The Agricultural Commissioner has made no finding of fault.

"6. Because staff members of ALRB have a history of anti-agribusiness bias, they should be considered suspect witnesses.

"7. Under the headline 'Tests Suggest Worker Exposed to Pesticides,' *The Californian* on July 21, 1982, reported there was a red blood cell count showing cells per cubic millimeter. This shows whether a person is anemic. It is not a measure of cholinesterase in the cells and has nothing to do with pesticide poisoning. I brought this to Mr. Engstrom's attention and he has done nothing to correct the public impression."[124] (The newspaper had published a correction and clarification of point 7 on July 30, 1982 two weeks prior to Cheatham's op-ed.)

The following month The Monterey County Board of Supervisors responded to Cheatham and Marshall's letters and informed Supervisor Marc Del Piero that "Dr. Velasco is no longer a county employee...[he] is now in private practice in Salinas. Like many local private physicians, he is on the medical staff of the hospital."[125]

The complaint from James Cheatham was thoroughly examined and discharged. The Natividad Hospital Administrator notified Cheatham by letter. "In accordance with usual and customary practice to determine professional competence of physicians granted medical staff privileges at Natividad Medical Center, letters dated July 22, 1982 and July 23, 1982, from James T. Cheatham and E. R. Marshall respectively were referred to the Credentials Committee of the Medical Staff for evaluation and response.

"First, the Credentials Committee feels it is important to note that Dr. Antonio Velasco is not a 'Monterey County

202

Employee' as stated by Mr. Cheatham's letter but rather is a member of the Medical Staff with privileges in Family medicine.

"The Credentials Committee has carefully reviewed the credentials and professional performance of Dr. Velasco and has found nothing which would support the allegations made in either of the letters in question.

"Obviously, the physician/patient relationship is privileged and since there has been no complaint from a patient, the Committee is of the opinion that it has insufficient information to warrant further investigation.

"If further review by the Committee is desired by your Board, the names of specific patients, including signed authorizations by patients, should be provided by the two individuals making the allegations."[126]

The petition did not deter Antonio. Natividad had to deal with a county bureaucracy that balked at providing funds for lab services unless they had assurances of reimbursement. Confronted with the issue of two children involved in the case, insurance companies hesitated making payments fearing that, as carriers for growers and harvesters providing health benefits, it could lead to charges of violating child labor law.

Antonio took time off from work in his clinic, facing false allegations, and continuing research on pesticides as the date for Isabel's delivery drew close. On October 15, 1982 she gave birth to Beatriz another baby girl.

In the world beyond the Maternity Department walls of Natividad an increasingly bitter internecine battle between growers and harvesters erupted with neither party willing to accept responsibility for covering workers. Farm hands did not receive Workers' Compensation or medical benefits in a clear violation of California Agricultural Regulations.[127]

Lack of earnings and the inability to receive funds for medical care as well as the hospital requiring reimbursement placed migrant farm workers in an untenable situation. They had to work in order to support their families.

Natividad physicians led by Antonio Velasco requested[128] Chief Medical Officer of Cal/OSHA, Dr. Ira Monossan, pressure insurance companies to pay worker compensation and medical costs. Although Cal/OSHA did not have authority to make legal demands on the companies, Monassan's research did prove invaluable in the court's decision to issue an injunction requiring the companies to remunerate workers for medical fees and lost wages.

Insurance firms appealed the injunction. The delay in compensation compelled a substantial number of workers to abandon medical treatment. Attorneys for CRLA and Cal/OSHA took action. The court rejected insurance company appeals and forced carriers to obey the order. They complied, and patients received worker compensation.

Doctors and hospitals recouped medical costs. Unfortunately the newly acquired knowledge of labor rights created a negative impact on workers. When they asked for dates of pesticide application in fields they were labeled as troublemakers and had difficulty gaining employment.

While cases wended their way through courts the State of California Department of Food and Agriculture issued reports with data gathered by the department, Cal/OSHA, and the Kern County Department of Agriculture detailing deaths and illnesses of farm workers directly related to pesticide exposure.

204

A devastating article in the *Annual Review Public Health* noted that powerful chemicals for killing pests raised concern they are agents of environmental pollution and human disease. The greatest concern involved potential delayed health effects of pesticide exposure, rather than the relatively well understood acute effects. The article listed three forms of cancer: leukemia, Hodgkin's lymphoma, and multiple myeloma as the most prevalent farmworker illnesses in the State of California caused by exposure to pesticides.[129]

The preponderance of evidence led to proposed changes in safety regulations for field hands and pesticide workers. The chemical industry, including applicators, came out in force opposing regulations and demanded that regulations be "loosened" rather than stringent.

California Governor George Deukmejian chose to ignore factual, scientific conclusions drawn by damaging reports of the California Department of Food and Agriculture. His office announced: "...it is the policy of his administration to reduce government intrusion in private affairs, and to stimulate economic growth by removing unneeded government regulations."[130]

The governor's support of the pesticide industry emboldened corporate entities fearful of requirements to erect shields to lower and/or prevent poisoning incidents. Battle lines hardened between those intent on protecting workers against serious illness and death and chemical manufacturers, pesticide applicators and agribusiness.

Ralph Lightstone and William Monning of California Rural Legal Assistance prepared comments on the proposed weaker amendments to pesticide worker safety regulations.

"California leads the nation in pesticide use, and in documented worker pesticide poisoning cases. It has also developed the most comprehensive pesticide regulations in the country. These amendments are the first worker safety regulation changes proposed by the new director of the CDFA [California Department of Food and Agriculture]. While they clarify and strengthen some provisions of existing law, the overall effect of these proposed amendments is to weaken existing regulations designed to protect workers from pesticide hazards, and to continue in effect weaknesses already contained in the regulations...

"...The poisoning of farmworkers and others during the past few years demonstrates the need to strengthen, not weaken, the pesticide program...

"...We are disappointed that the department has once again neglected to establish a statewide posting program for the one to six-day materials."[131]

The Natividad team developed documentation and statistical data combined with verifiable research that furnished sufficient grounds for CRLA under Bill Monning to pursue the case to the United States District Court of the Northern District of California.

Filed on September 15, 1983 CRLA made a demand for a jury trial. The complaint: personal injuries and wrongful death. The attorney of record was Alfred Lombardo of Rucka, O'Boyle & Lombardo in Salinas, California. Bill Monning and Ralph Lightstone from the Sacramento office represented CRLA.

Thirty-four plaintiffs sued Mobay Chemical Corporation, Admiral Packing Company, E.I. DuPont de Nemours Company, Fanciful Company, Aaron P. Moreno, Sr. and Soilserv, Inc.

A plaintiff in the suit, Maria Meca Flores, was poisoned by highly toxic chemicals within the first trimester of her pregnancy on approximately Sept. 18, 1982. Mrs. Flores gave birth to a baby girl, Marianna Flores on May 30, 1983. The infant suffered severe birth defects and died within two weeks. The suit alleged exposure to pesticides caused injuries to the fetus and the death of the child.[132]

Newspapers reported the case as it progressed through court. "A study showing a widely-used pesticide may cause birth defects has California agriculture officials worried...A San Francisco television station reported Wednesday that a confidential study completed in 1979 but only sent to the [California] Food and Agriculture Department last fall said the chemical may cause birth defects including brain damage... Under state law, pesticide safety tests are not public because chemical companies contend their disclosure would reveal trade secrets...Ralph Lightstone, an attorney with California Rural Legal Assistance in Sacramento, said environmental groups will likely seek a ban on Metasystox-R.

" 'My reaction is that it should be off the market'," he said.

"...A Mobay [Chemical Corporation] spokeswoman started: 'If the material is used in accordance with federal label requirements, we have no concerns about the safety of the material'.

"Monning [CRLA] said it is 'putting the cart before the horse' to allow the use of pesticides without adequate safety tests... 'They're waiting for tests on rabbits while, in the meantime, farm workers are guinea pigs,' he said."[133]

One year later the preponderance of evidence compiled in the pioneering research by Antonio Velasco and other Natividad physicians prompted the court to award a settlement of $278,000 to all affected farm workers. The Flores family received $40,000.

An article in the Salinas *Californian* reported "'The Flores' attitude throughout has been that no amount of money can make up for the loss of their child, but hopefully it will protect other lives'…At a press conference today, Mr. Flores said he still feels pain from the loss of his daughter, but added 'What good does anger do at this point? One does feel bad when something like this happens to a family, but maybe there will be more precautions taken.'…District Court Judge Robert Aguilar in San José presided over the settlement conference.

"In 1982, an out-of-court settlement of $202,000 was made in a suit stemming from an earlier pesticide poisoning case."[134]

Chapter Seventeen

Challenge and Vindication

Within weeks of the out-of-court settlement anonymous threatening phone calls to Antonio at the clinic and hospital warned that his family would come to harm if he did not halt his "anti-pesticide crusade." The medical facilities reported the threats to the police. Their response: they were powerless since no one had taken overt action and callers could not be identified.

One call changed the tenor of intimidations. A voice on the other end of the line benignly said "This is Danny from Las Vegas. Is Isabel home?" Antonio asked the caller what he wanted. After a few seconds the caller spat out, "Fuck you. Go back where you came from."

The message revealed a sinister dark side hidden behind the façade of the genteel conservative agricultural community. Antonio attempted to shield Isabel and his daughters but could not halt public pronouncements labeling him a self-aggrandizing troublemaker. His opponents continued to level emotionally charged false claims and lies against him in order to gain public support for their positions. Pro-pesticide efforts failed as newspapers, radio, and television reported facts not rumor; data not speculation.

Charlie Clements who had become a target for assassination by the U.S. funded right-wing militia in El Salvador escaped undercover and returned to the United States in order to complete his residency at Natividad. News of his mission in Central America as well as his work with Antonio's medical team raised his profile.

Ominous phone calls warned Clements he did not have long to live if he continued working at Natividad. His concerns abated when intimidating messages threatened his non-existent children. It became apparent to Clements that his anonymous callers had no idea where he lived or his lifestyle.

Harsh and accusatory attacks persisted against Antonio in the press, radio and television. Mounting scientific evidence that pesticides had detrimental effects on field workers countered the assault on facts. Incontrovertible proof substantiated the need to expand worker protection.

Ted Rose the dynamic chief of Natividad's Internal Medical Department threw the hospital's resources behind the increasingly larger group of scientists developing protocols to identify pesticide poisoning.

Farmworkers who experienced cholinesterase inhibition from exposure to organophosphates exhibited tiredness, weakness, dizziness, nausea and blurred vision, headache, sweating, tearing, drooling, vomiting, tunnel vision, and twitching within four to twenty-four hours of contact.

A majority of patients presented symptoms of abdominal cramps, involuntary urination, diarrhea, muscular tremors, staggering gait, pinpoint pupils, hypotension (abnormally low blood pressure), slow heartbeat and breathing difficulty. Death could occur if not promptly treated by a physician.[135]

James Cheatham led the opposition unleashing a propaganda barrage to discredit science and medical data that built a strong case against their interests.

In October 1982 Cheatham launched a last-ditch effort to thwart the avalanche of scientific evidence proving that pesticides had wrought havoc on field workers and neighborhoods surrounding suspect farms and orchards.

He wrote another letter in the Public Forum of the Salinas *Californian* stating: "I have been handling pesticides for over twenty years. My health and that of my employees has been monitored by competent physicians during all this time. Down through the years we have received [sic] constant, heavy exposure to pesticides. We are intimately familiar with the subject. Please pardon me if I find it ludicrous when a claim is made which in my knowledge and experience, could not be supported.

"In my letter to the Salinas *Californian* dated July 27, the following short paragraph was omitted:

" 'The doctor [Antonio Velasco] who diagnosed the ALRB people has a history of hospitalizing people who have been released by other, very competent doctors.'

"Just think of the potential, where a doctor who is an anti-pesticide activist is in a position to put his politics ahead of his medicine.

"This is the same doctor who, representing the United Farm Workers, hospitalized fourteen workers last year, [sic] after they had been given a clean bill of healthy by other doctors. It's the same guy who told Bob Johnson's employee he was poisoned, when in fact he had the flu. He's the same one who told the lady at Boronda Adobe that her kids were poisoned but failed to report the evidence to the Health Department as required by law. He is active with UFW, is at least partially supported by government grants, and his pesticide diagnoses seem always to get big media play.

"Yes, I am concerned about 'suspect witnesses'. The Salinas *Californian* has tried and condemned my company by innuendo. I challenge these ALRB people to follow through on their public threat and sue me. If they do, maybe they will be exposed to the light of day."[136]

"It was all over the news," Isabel recalled. "I knew the reports were not true. Cheatham misquoted Antonio and Charlie Clements. He claimed they were putting on a circus. Our children wanted to know what their father was doing. I explained it to them, and we were all supportive. I did become frightened when Cheatham called Antonio a rabble-rouser.

"At the time I worked with a local school as a social worker to develop a plan for parents to become involved in the educational system. The school board sided with the growers. I received calls at home from men and women who told me to be careful if I had any more meetings with parents. They knew I had children. They knew where Antonio worked. After that every time the phone rang I became rattled. Charlie Clements stayed with us and thankfully nothing happened."

Antonio pulled an old, yellowing journal from a file and read an entry he made four months before the pesticide incident.

"March 6, 1980. Isabel had a big hassle at work. She was very upset. She wants to talk to me immediately. I didn't realize how heavily I rely on her for support until she needs my support. It's natural for us to be strong. We work together."

Cheatham's allegations against Antonio strengthened the physician's resolve. Antonio emphasized to his lawyer that every point made by Cheatham "is untrue, defamatory, libelous and actionable." His attorney John A. Burgess, Berkeley, California forwarded a Notice and Demand for Retraction of Defamatory Statements from the Salinas *Californian* and its parent company Gannett News Service.

Antonio Velasco, MD. Pesticide investigation laboratory, 1981.
(Monterey Herald)

The research team at Natividad reviewed all the extant literature dealing with pesticide poisoning during their treatment of patients. They collated data while care of ill farm workers continued. Statistics proved Antonio's theory

213

of cholinesterase regeneration. It led to a breakthrough in identifying symptoms and possible outcomes and had an impact on physicians and researchers for years.

In 1985 the Natividad team published peer-reviewed results of treatment and research into organophosphate poisoning with information from Clements' Masters thesis. The report included detailed analyses of patients over a period of eleven to one hundred twenty-six days of exposure to organophosphate insecticides with a clear and well-documented graph of symptoms. The report ended with a summary of poisoning incidents and the positive outcome of the Monterey County hearing.

"The possible hazards of this occupation [cauliflower harvesting] were underscored when a second tying crew was poisoned in September 1982. Of the thirty-six persons poisoned in this second incident, 6 were among the patients included in this report. A third cauliflower crew was poisoned in the Salinas Valley in April 1983.

"In response to the problem of residue-induced illness, Monterey County has adopted a unique regulation requiring worker safety reentry interval of 24 hours or greater is in effect."[137]

James Cheatham's attempt to defame and silence Antonio with false accusations and blatant misinformation about his credentials and professional expertise came to an abrupt halt when the Monterey County Department of Health discovered leaking pesticide containers on Cheatham property draining beyond the Verticare facility on May 3, 1984. Toxic chemicals killed vegetation growing on adjacent land. Polluted pesticide containers had been disposed illegally at a sanitary landfill. Analyses of contaminated soil, waste material from

214

a dumpster and unknown liquids leaking from containers confirmed the presence of noxious pesticides.

The California Department of Health Services held his company, Verticare, responsible for releasing pesticides into the environment. The department issued a Remedial Action Order for Verticare.[138]

In a letter dated August 1, 1984 the department requested that Cheatham individually and as president of Verticare submit a Plan of Correction within thirty days. Cheatham failed to respond. He may have believed supporters would quash the request.

The department sent another request to Verticare on October 5, 1984. Once more Cheatham ignored the petition. Government officials reacted by notifying that his company, Verticare, had been placed on the State Superfund list of hazardous sites. The harsh warning caught Cheatham's attention. He responded with a plea to permit his company to handle the situation on its own. Department of Health judged the hasty plan Cheatham produced to ameliorate the problem as insufficient.

The court ordered Verticare and Cheatham on July 21, 1986 to implement a Remedial Action Plan (RAP) prepared by outside engineers. Failure or refusal to comply with the order would make the company and owners liable for all costs in the event of remedial action of the site.

Chapter Eighteen

Reward

February 1992, Salinas, California

Antonio Velasco pulled on his trademark cowboy boots and dressed for another busy day at Val Verde Medical Clinic. He glanced out a window at vast acres of freshly plowed rich, dark earth and recalled the harsh years toiling with his family in the fields. Within months farm workers from Mexico, Central America and South America would swarm to the fields for the harvest. Antonio felt a close kinship to those men and women who trusted him for their medical care.

The aroma of freshly brewed coffee greeted him in the breakfast room. Isabel packed school lunches for thirteen-year-old Anisvel and her ten-year old sister Beatriz. The baby of the family, four-year old Tizoc sat on Antonio's lap.

The Salinas Christian School bus rolled up to the house. The girls hoisted their backpacks, kissed their mother and father goodbye and dashed outside. Isabel prepared to drop off Tizoc at pre-school before going to work as manager of Antonio's clinic.

She handed Antonio a copy of the calendar for the coming week. "Not too busy except for babies due on Tuesday

216

and Wednesday. You have a full patient schedule. The Rendóns are coming on Monday. *Doña* Carmen Zarco wants to see you on Thursday. She's having a problem with her legs."

"I'm taking a group of residents from Natividad to visit a labor camp Thursday afternoon. I plan to check out the kids and some of the old folks. Ask *Doña* Carmen to come in before ten," suggested Antonio.

"Do you have notes for your radio program on Sunday evening?" asked Isabel.

"It's the same every week. A teenager's going to call and ask what to do about the zit on his or her nose," he laughed.

The calendar for the following month had two weeks marked off. The family planned a two-week trip to his hometown of Cofradía de Suchitlán. Antonio and Isabel renovated the stone house of his childhood with modern additions created out of brick and iron designed by local artisans. It served as headquarters for a foundation partially funded by Rotary International providing university scholarships for qualified Mexican high school students.

He had broken the cycle of life repeated day after day, week after week, and year after year by typical farmworkers with the power of his intellect and talent even when deep doubts from his harsh childhood intruded on reality.

Isabel was the only person to whom he registered those fears. She supported his decisions knowing that the Antonio Velasco filled with doubt was the small eleven-year-old boy who crossed the border a lifetime ago. As a dedicated scientist, researcher, and physician he gained the respect of the medical community and society. The California Academy of Family Physicians notified Antonio he was on the list of nominees for

Physician of the Year. He felt it was a long shot and did not plan on attending the annual conference.

"I kept receiving phone calls from the Academy requesting that I appear with the other nominees. At the time I thought it was routine protocol," recalled Antonio.

He reminisced commenting to Isabel: "It looks as if the Academy's having difficulty getting members to attend its meeting."

"You ought to go. You might learn something new," suggested Isabel.

"I have too much work. My patients expect me to be there for them," said Antonio.

"You don't have to be away for long. Fly to San Diego after your last patient on Thursday. Stay for the Friday sessions and return on Saturday. The other doctors at the clinic can take over for one day. You'll enjoy being with friends. Jeff Solinas will probably be there. Maybe some of the others—Jim Coleman for example," said Isabel.

Antonio reviewed his schedule. "I'm on call for the weekend."

"Go for the day. It's quick flight. You'll be back on Friday in time for dinner," Isabel insisted.

Late Thursday afternoon he drove southwest on State Highway 68 past one of the premier sports car racing venues in California the Laguna Seca Raceway and up to Monterey Peninsula Airport situated incongruously on a mesa with a sheer drop at the end of the runway.

Antonio marveled that aircraft never tumbled off the edge into an abyss. Pilots adroitly made safe departures and that afternoon was no different. The Southwest 737 made the trip to San Diego in two and a half hours including a brief layover in San Francisco. Antonio arrived at his hotel just as lightning and thunder struck the resort city. Any thought of basking in the sunshine of pleasant sunny Southern California vanished in the clatter of rain beating against windows.

"When I registered for the conference the clerk seemed excited and told me that I should let her know my room number as soon as I registered," said Antonio. "I received a phone call in my room from the secretary of the awards committee. She told me I had been selected to receive the honor." The unexpected notification dumbfounded him. "I had to sit down and let it sink in while she instructed me on the schedule of activities. It all happened so fast and unexpectedly that my head was turning."

The Academy planned a brief ceremony for the award early in the afternoon. A luncheon was planned for the following day. He wished he could share the moment with family and friends. Antonio called Isabel and expressed his anxiety at the academy's decision. She reassured him he deserved the honor and to enjoy every moment.

After attending sessions devoted to current medical issues and updates on medical insurance, he joined several friends for lunch. The Academy formally requested him not reveal his selection. Antonio made small talk as the others opined on who the 1992 honoree would be. They bandied names of prominent university doctors, researchers from established institutions, and physicians from urban areas of California.

After lunch Antonio entered the large meeting room. An Academy aide ushered him to a reserved seat on the aisle. The president of the academy came to the end of a lengthy series of awards and certificates of appreciation.

"This year, the Academy is proud to present the California Physician of the Year award to a physician who made an enormous contribution to medicine not only in California but in the United States. His work and research has had a major impact in the field of preventive medicine. I am proud to announce that the 1992 California Family Physician of the Year is Antonio R. Velasco of Salinas.

"In 1991 Antonio R. Velasco received the University of California Alumni Association Humanitarian Award," continued the president. "He co-founded the Salvadoran Medical Relief Fund. Without a doubt his work and research was critical to the passage of landmark legislation to protect workers against pesticide poisoning. His research led him to establish the Natividad Medical Center Farmworker Pesticide Treatment Clinic in Salinas, California. Ladies and gentlemen, Antonio R. Velasco."

Antonio walked to the dais and looked over the gathering of brown, black, Asian, Native American and white doctors reflecting the vast diversity of physicians in California. A clap of thunder stirred long-buried memories of *Volcán de Fuego* and the arduous trek he took as a small, skinny boy from a distant village high in the mountains of Mexico to the mysterious *El Norte* of mythology and dreams.

Antonio Velasco continued providing both free and low-cost medical care to farm workers throughout the Salinas Valley and surrounding areas. He lectures throughout the United States on the dangers of pesticides. Universities invite him to present seminars for students majoring in public health on protocols for identifying and diagnosing the effects of toxic chemicals.

His articles appear in peer reviewed medical journals providing health care professionals with information expanded from the initial investigation of pesticide poisoning incidents in Salinas fields.

Twenty-six years after receiving the Physician of the Year award from the California Academy of Family Physicians the birth of *Clínica Tepati* remained one of the major milestone events in Antonio Velasco's life.

On May 12, 2018 Antonio Velasco, M.D. returned to Davis Medical School for *Clínica Tepati's* 44th anniversary. The administrators of the clinic invited him to give the keynote address in which he encapsulated his ideal vision for providing medical care.

"Forty-two years ago… in my second year of medical school at UCD [I] was elected Chairman of the *Clínica Tepati* Board of Directors… The *Clínica* was operating out of a legal services office in Sacramento… The summer I became chairman I contacted the Sacramento County Public Health Director. It had come to our attention that there was a county clinic operating in our area. I negotiated a contract for *Clínica* to use this facility on Saturdays, when it was normally closed. This simple act transformed *Clínica* . We now had access to a fully stocked facility and could concentrate all our efforts to provide quality medical care. In the process, we were all learning not just about medicine but enhancing our ability to deliver quality medical services to our community.

"My plan, when I decided to pursue a medical career, was to return to my community to serve the farm worker population with whom I had grown up… I went to the Natividad Medical Center Family Practice Residency, in Salinas, California. This is the Monterey County Hospital

221

in southern Monterey County where my family settled after years of migrant farm labor.

"My biggest challenge however was my involvement with treating patients who were poisoned by pesticides... We were in for a fight...[However] We became the leading authority in the field of pesticide treatment of farm workers...

"I learned [that] success is a journey, not a destination. Viewed in this manner it allows you to live in the moment and view any failure not as a defeat but simply a minor delay in that journey. Also, success requires daily effort and as long as you are involved in the process you are being successful. Don't give up!

"Three elements of a successful medical provider, in order of importance: Availability. In private practice it means having access to you 24/7.

"But I think the concept of 'availability' goes beyond the physical realm. Being available means having good communication with patients, looking them in the eyes, listening carefully, examining them as we elicit their history before turning our attention to the monitor and entering data.

"Affability. In a hospital setting patients are usually treated impersonally. While making rounds we speak of them in the third person, as though they are not there. When people are ill and scared they need a friendly face; someone who smiles at them and conveys a caring attitude.

"In my twenty-three years of practice, delivering about thirty babies a month, I was never sued. All this while treating the highest-risk migrant farm worker population. Much of this is due to affability, the art of connecting with patients and conveying that you care. We are all well trained in the science

222

and practice of medicine. It is up to us to sensitize ourselves to be thoughtful and considerate.

"Ability. We must learn as much as possible to provide the best care. But we must remain aware of our shortcomings and elicit consultations when in doubt. Always try to know what you don't know and refer to someone who does."

EPILOGUE

by Antonio Velasco, M.D.

Deep within I always believed my story was not particularly unusual. The unexpected opinion of others forced guttural, relentless memories to emerge. I arrived in the United States as an immigrant, a child from a small village. Racism and fear of the other existed in my new home but it did not hold me back from achieving along with multitudes of immigrants who gave their talent and intellect to improve life in America. Times have changed. We live at a critical time when the word "immigrant" has a negative slant.

The cry "Go back home" aimed at the stranger in our midst echoes across the cities and plains of our democracy contradicting the poem written by another immigrant Emma Lazarus engraved in bronze on the Statue of Liberty: "Send these, the homeless, tempest-tost to me, I lift my lamp beside the golden door!"

I achieved beyond my wildest dreams. But credit must be equally shared. The collective "we" prevailed in our fight to defend the underserved that had little or no political voice. A cadre of individuals are the "we" who came together united for one purpose: to make working, living and health conditions safer for farmworkers. Success was only possible with a group effort led by professionals such as Dr. Charlie Clements and national experts in the field of pesticide illness

224

treatment; brilliant lawyers like Bill Monning now a California State Senator; community workers, organizers, activists; and, most of all hard-working farmworkers. From the bottom of my heart I thank all my friends and co-workers for giving me credit more than I deserve.

Our children have become successful in business, medicine, and education. Like my daughters and son, I have a passion for work. Unlike them, my early years had great challenges. I believed my future was going to be better, much better. America, after all, was the land of opportunity. I also knew that education was the best route to success. Armed with this conviction, I embarked on an arduous journey of discovery.

My development took on a life of its own. I often felt in the right place, with the right people, at the right time. I also realized that actions, attitudes, and those with whom we interact determine destiny. I resolved to do something positive and meaningful with my life. As an immigrant I viewed every challenge as an opportunity not an obstacle.

The decision to enter the medical profession did not come from the heavens as an apotheosis. Mentors and events shaped my future. My mother collapsed during a tomato harvest when I was twelve-years old. The heartless, uncaring reaction of local emergency rooms and clinics who refused to treat her had an enormous, angry impact on my psyche. In contrast the care she received at Natividad Medical Center in Salinas demonstrated there were medical professionals who cared. In retrospect that incident may have been an unconscious trigger toward my decision.

The first time I considered seriously studying medicine was in high school. My Spanish teacher suggested I go abroad to medical school. At the time, it seemed an unattainable goal, but the idea came alive. As a freshman science student at the University of California, Santa Cruz I volunteered at a farm workers clinic. That experience clinched my decision to pursue a medical career.

A turning point came in 1980 when I joined a community group hoping to organize a farmworker clinic in Salinas. I met Cesar Chavez, one of the founders of the United Farm Workers, at that meeting. I asked what he thought was the greatest health risk facing farm workers. Without hesitation he answered it was pesticides. I left the meeting feeling as if I had a mission.

The critical goal in my professional life became the protection of farm workers against the invidious, toxic impact of chemicals that disables, maims, and kills women, men, and children who inadvertently come into contact with noxious pesticides.

Throughout my life I had excellent teachers, from my father, who was the hardest worker I have ever known, to my mother who supported my education wholeheartedly. Schoolteachers took special interest in me and determined my future opportunities. Employers supported my efforts and rewarded me with responsibilities beyond the usual scope given to adolescents. Administrators in all the educational institutions I attended assisted my activities and projects.

My wife and the whole village surrounding me every step of the way provided encouragement. With their support, guidance, and encouragement they prodded me to pursue my career as a health provider. They also gave me impetus to lift up those who have little political power when faced with harm from unethical corporate interests.

226

Cofradía de Suchitlán. Isabel & Antonio, 2014. (M. Halperin)

Cofradía Cemetery, 2014. Antonio & Isabel Velasco at the gravesite of Antionio's father, José Dolores Velasco, and his grandfather, Jesús Velasco Ávalos. His mother's ashes are buried with his father. (M. Halperin)

ANTONIO VELASCO, M.D.

The University of California Santa Cruz Division of Physical and Biological Sciences presented the PBSci Distinguished Alumni award to Dr. Velasco in October 2018 for his pioneering work in the management of pesticide exposure. He and Isabel were co-founders of the Salvadoran Medical Relief Fund with Charlie Clements. He also works with the International Medical Relief Fund providing health care, medicine, and medical supplies to communities in El Salvador and Mexico.

Dr. Velasco founded *Clínica Popular*, a nonprofit community clinic in Salinas, California. He continues lecturing on the dangers of pesticides and public health issues surrounding pesticide regulation reform. His childhood home in Cofradía de Suchitlán has become the center of the Velasco's philanthropic programs. The stone house where he was born serves as his study and library. For recreation Dr. Velasco grows coffee in Cofradía de Suchitlán that he roasts and presents as gifts to friends and acquaintances.

ISABEL GUZMÁN-VELASCO

Isabel retired with Antonio and was instrumental in developing the university scholarship program for Mexican high school students. Isabel's prime job is teaching her first grandchild the morals and values that molded her life.

MEYO (REMEDIOS) VELASCO-LÓPEZ

Antonio's oldest sister retired from her position as executive assistant at UC Santa Cruz in 2015. She assists members of her church with translations, transportation to medical centers, and helps the elderly and those not conversant with English complete legal forms.

ANISVEL (ANIS) VELASCO SALVESEN

Antonio and Isabel's eldest daughter received her BA degree in French Literature from Brown University, Providence, Rhode Island. She has an MBA granted by the Monterey Institute of International Studies. Anis holds the executive post of global marketing director for a major corporation in San Francisco. She is married and presented her parents with their first grandchild.

BEATRIZ VELASCO

Beatriz, the Velasco's middle child, earned her BA degree in Biology and a Registered Nurse degree from California State University, San José. Beatriz is a trauma center surgical nurse and active in the Hispanic Nurses Association where she was treasurer.

TIZOC VELASCO

Antonio and Isabel's son received his BA in Environmental Studies, University of California, Santa Barbara. He earned his teaching credential in biology from California State University, Monterey Bay. Tizoc teaches high school biology.

JOSÉ DOLORES VELASCO CHÁVEZ (1926-1993)

Antonio Velasco's father, a corn farmer from Cofradia de Suchitlan, Colima, Mexico, joined thousands of Mexican men in the Bracero guest worker program in 1953 and traveled to the citrus orchards of Yuma, Arizona, north of the border where he became an expert in irrigation methods and installation. A rancher hired Jose full time keeping him in Arizona for extended periods of time. Jose eventually arranged documentation permitting his family entry into the United States. Eager to increase his earning power, he brought them to California where they traveled the migrant farmworker trail for the annual harvests. With his son David's assistance he obtained a permanent position driving a forklift. He retired with a guaranteed pension and Social Security benefits. He is buried in the Cofradía cemetery alongside his father Jesus Velasco Ávalos.

TERESA RAMÍREZ VELASCO (1934-2012)

Born in Hacienda Nogueras, Colima, Mexico, Antonio Velasco's mother served the village and the area surrounding Cofradia de Suchitlan with the aid of the Mexican Health Department as an herbalist and community health adviser. Upon entering the United States with her children, Teresa worked side-by-side with her husband in the fields. Eventually she joined Jose and her older son David at a garlic and onion processing plant in King City, California. Teresa retired after twenty years with pension and Social Security benefits. Her ashes are buried with her husband in Cofradia.

DAVID VELASCO

Antonio's older brother, born in 1949, graduated from The Commercial Industrial Technical Academy in San Luis Rio Colorado planning to work in finance. Forced by his father to join him as a farmworker, David worked in the fields for twenty years. With his principal ambition thwarted, he turned to engineering. He became a successful diesel mechanic and semi-truck driver. With Isabel's agreement Antonio turned over his Natividad Hospital residency pension to David as a down payment on a diesel truck in order to provide for his brother's independence. He retired to Texas with his wife Berta.

Reference Notes and Sources

CHAPTER ONE—Consequence

[1]   Armstrong, V.I., *I Have Spoken*. Sage Books, The Swallow Press, 1971. Pgs. 56-57.

[2]   Delay, B. *Independent Indians and the U.S. Mexican War*. The American Historical Review, Vol. 112, Issue 1, Feb. 1, 2007. Pgs. 35-68.

[3]   Nester, W.R. *The Age of Jackson and the Art of American Power, 1815-1848*. Potomac Books, Washington, D.C. 2013.

[4]   *Appendix to the Congressional Globe, 29th Congress, 1st Session*. July 14, 1846. Page 828.

[5]   Peters, R., ed., *The Public Statutes at Large of the United States of America*, v.5, pp. 797-798. Little and Brown, Boston. 1850.

[6]   Polk, J.K. *War with Mexico*. Address to Congress 1846.

[7]   Hopkins, J.F. *The Papers of Henry Clay: Candidate, Compromiser, Elder Statesman*. University of Kentucky Press, 1963.

8   Kluger, R. *Seizing Destiny: How America Grew from Sea to Shining Sea*. Knopf, New York. 2007.

9   Roosevelt, F.D. First Inaugural Address, March 4, 1933.

10   Roosevelt, F.D. *Address at Chautauqua, New York*, August 14, 1936.

11   The Mexican Farm Labor program called "For the Temporary Migration of Mexican Agricultural Workers to the United States as Revised on April 26, 1943, by an Exchange of Notes Between the American Embassy at Mexico City and the Mexican Ministry for Foreign Affairs."

12   Koestler, Fred L. *Operation Wetback*, Handbook of Texas Online, Texas Historical Assn., June 15, 2010.

13   1951 Public Law 78: Extension of the Bracero Program. S. 984; Pub. L. 82-78; 65 Stat. 119. 82nd Congress; July 12, 1951.

14   Kibbe, P. R. *Latin Americans in Texas*. University of New Mexico Press, Albuquerque, New Mexico, 1948.

CHAPTER TWO—Under the Volcano

15   Cofradía de Suchitlán (Association of Suchitlán). Cofradía often used as a prefix in Mexico for villages formed by related families.

[16]   Fred L. Koestler. *"Operation Wetback."* Handbook of Texas Online. Texas State Historical Assn. Mar. 25, 2016.

[17]   Los Angeles Committee for Protection of Foreign Born Records, 1938-1973 (Southern California Library for Social Studies and Research)

[18]   Gutiérrez, David G. *Walls and Mirrors: Mexican Americans, Mexican Immigrants, and the Politics of Ethnicity.* University of California Press, 1995. Page 175.

[19]   The Alien Registration Receipt Card (USCIS Form I-151), commonly called the "Green Card", is an identification card attesting to permanent resident status of an alien in the United States. The card has gone through multiple versions, the latest introduced in 2010.

[20]   Portuguese settled in Mexico in the late 16th century and throughout the 17th century when Spain and Portugal were one kingdom. For the most part they assimilated into Mexican culture and society.

[21]   *Guardadito* a term commonly translated as a hidden place for readily available cash.

CHAPTER THREE—San Luis Colorado

[22]   The Sonoran Desert in northwestern Mexico is the driest and hottest desert in Mexico and covers a large part of Southwestern United States.

²³ San Luis Rio Colorado lies on the international border of the United States in the northwest corner of the State of Sonora, Mexico.

CHAPTER FOUR—A Hint of Sand

²⁴ *51 Wet Mexicans.* Yuma Daily Sun, April 30, 1953. P. 3.

²⁵ John F. Kennedy Address, Mexico City, Mexico, June 29, 1962.

²⁶ Nogales, Arizona is one of the principal Ports of Entry into the United States from Mexico.

²⁷ Somerton, Arizona lies north of San Luis Rio Colorado approximately twelve miles south of Yuma, Arizona.

²⁸ The 90-mile long Salinas Valley runs north to south is one of the most productive agricultural regions of California and has the sobriquet "Salad Bowl of the World."

CHAPTER FIVE—The American Dream

²⁹ Greenfield, California located in Monterey County's Salinas Valley produces the majority of broccoli consumed in the United States.

CHAPTER SIX—Friendship and Faith

[30] Tranquilino Rendón, Jr. (Kili) owns and operates an electric repair company in Northern California.

[31] Natividad Hospital established in Monterey County in 1844 became the county hospital in 1886. According to their mission statement the hospital is dedicated "To monitor and improve the health of the people, including the vulnerable through coordinated, affordable, high quality care."

CHAPTER SEVEN-Wheels

[32] Pinnacles National Monument established in 1905 was named a national park in 2013.

[33] California Scholarship Foundation recognizes California students who demonstrate high levels of academic achievement.

[34] Dust Bowl: a period of severe drought in the 1930s resulted in severe dust storms. The lengthy period of drought impacted the Great Depression created vast migrations of families in search of work.

[35] Clayton Abajian served in the Air Force during the Vietnam War encrypting code. He earned his Bachelor's Degree from the Division of Nursing, California State University Sacramento and retired as the Asst. Nurse Manager, Dept. of Radiology, UC Davis Medical Center.

36   Walter F. Mondale served as senator from Minnesota (1964-1976). Elected Vice-President of the United States (1977-1981). He was the Democratic nominee for president (1984).

37   Subcommittee on Migratory Labor of the Committee on Labor and Public Welfare, United States Senate, 95th Congress, First and Second Sessions on Farmworker Legal Problems. August 8, 1969.

38   Aldrin was banned from use in 1999 due to its toxicity to marine life including fish and mammals.

39   Irma West, M.D. (1917-2017) worked for the California Department of Public Health primarily in occupational medicine and toxicology including research and investigation into the health effects of pesticides on agricultural workers.

40   *Hearings Before the Subcommittee on Migratory Labor of the Committee on Labors and Public Welfare, United States Senate.* Ninety-First Congress. First Session on Efforts to Organize. July 15, 1969, Part 3-A.

41   The Wagner-Peyser Act of 1933 provided "for the establishment of a national employment system and for cooperation with the States in the promotion of such system, and for other purposes established a nationwide system of public employment offices."

42   *Hearings Before the Subcommittee on Migratory Labor of the Committee on Labor and Public Welfare, United States Senate.* Ninety-First Congress. First and Second Sessions on Manpower and Economic Problems. April 15, 1970. Part 7-B.

43   Petit, C. *Dow Assails DBCP Pesticide's Critics.* San Francisco Chronicle, Oct. 19, 1977. p. 20.

CHAPTER NINE—Specter of Bigotry

44   The Education Opportunity program (EOP) provides services to low-income, historically educationally disadvantaged, and first-generation college students.

45   Cecilia Velasco graduated from Stanford University. Josefina Velasco graduated from the University of California, Santa Barbara.

46   MEChA: Acronym for *Moviemento Estudiantil Chicano de Aztlán* (Chicano Student Movement of Aztlán) founded in 1960 at the University of California, Santa Barbara.

47   Rita Solinas (1931-2007) MA, Psychology, University of California, Santa Barbara; Counseling Psychologist, University of California, Santa Cruz; recipient of Ford Fellowship, U.C. Santa Barbara.

48   Self-Help International headquartered in Waverly, Iowa works to alleviate hunger by assisting rural

poor, small-scale farmers and related enterprises in developing countries.

49   VFW Magazine and the Public Information Office, HQ CP Forward Observer-1st Recon April 12, 1997.

50   City on a Hill Press, University of California Santa Cruz. Nov. 6, 1972.

CHAPTER TEN—*El Amor Todo lo Puede*

51   James E. Coleman, M.D. is affiliated with Kaiser-Permanente, Orange County, California.

52   William Monning worked as staff attorney for the United Farm Workers of America from 1976 to 1978. From 1978 to 1982 he was Directing Attorney for California Rural Legal Assistance, Migrant Farm Worker Project. He was also Director of the Salvadoran Medical Relief Fund, and Executive Director for International Physicians for the Prevention of Nuclear War. In 2012 Monning was elected to the California State Senate and became Senate Majority leader in 2014. He was reelected to the Senate in 2016 for a second term.

53   Dana Kent and Bill Monning married after she graduated Harvard Medical School. Dr. Kent did her residency in 1991 at Natividad Medical Center before entering private practice in Monterey County, California.

54   Statement by the Religious, Civic and Labor Leaders, April 10, 1973.

[55]   Turner, W. *Teamsters Sued by* Chávez's *Union.* New York Times, Jan. 5, 1973. P. 4

[56]   Kenneth Thimann (1904—1997) eminent plant physiologist and microbiologist was the first Provost of Crown College, U.C. Santa Cruz

[57]   Title VI of the Civil Rights Act of 1964, 42 U.S.C. 2000d et seq. ("Title VI") Title VI prohibits discrimination on the basis of race, color, or national origin in any program or activity that receives Federal funds or other Federal financial assistance.

[58]   Decision in Superior Court of California, Nov. 20, 1974.

CHAPTER ELEVEN—Medical School

[59]   Antonio Ruelas earned his M.D. from the University of California Davis School of Medicine in 1978. Dr. Ruelas practices Family Medicine in Santa Paula, California.

[60]   Frank Meza (1950-2019) received his M.D. from the University of California Davis School of Medicine in 1978. The child of Mexican immigrants, he made a major impact on bringing Latinos into the medical professions.

[61]   Griswold del Castillo, R.; García, R. A. *César Chávez: A Triumph of Spirit.* University of Oklahoma Press; Revised edition (September 15, 1995) Pages 129-130.

[62] Librium is primarily used by those suffering from severe and debilitating anxiety disorders.

[63] UCDavis Medicine: A UC Davis School of Medicine publication for alumni, friends and physicians. *2002 Humanitarian-Bruce Greenburg, M.D.* Spring 2003.

[64] California Medi-Corps utilizes medical students to provide direct health and welfare services to migrant children and families.

[65] Smilkstein, G. *Ghetto America and developing world health care delivery* (Community Medicine). Calif. Med 118:94-97, Apr. 1973.

[66] *Medical Students Examine Minority Program*, San Francisco Chronicle, Thurs., Nov. 18, 1976. Page 4.

[67] Memo *"The impact of task force students on the curriculum"* from Dr. Donal Walsh, Dept. of Biological Chemistry, School of Medicine, University of California Davis to Dr. E. Gardner, Chairman CEP. October 10, 1975.

[68] Memo. Ernest Gardner, M.D. to Course Managers and Department and Division Chairmen. December 3, 1975

[69] Loretta Ortiz y Piño (1954-2017) earned her M.D. from Stanford University. She officiated as Holy Cross Hospital's Chief Medical Officer, Taos, New Mexico from 2011-2015.

[70] Supreme Court of California, Sept. 16, 1976. Bakk*e*, 18 Cal. 3d at 55.

[71] *AREAP Statement on Bakke Decision*. Synapse, the UCSF student newspaper. Vol. 21, No. 20, March 3, 1977.

[72] Federal Bureau of Health Professions assists in reducing imbalances in the health workforce that lead to disparity and lack of access in areas, populations or facilities with chronic difficulties attracting health care providers to meet their manpower needs.

[73] American Medical Students Assn. (AMSA), founded in 1950 is a student-governed, national organization committed to representing the concerns of physicians-in-training.

[74] Charlie Clements, MD, MPH wrote *Witness to War: An American Doctor in El Salvador,* Bantam Books, 1984. The book was produced as a documentary that won the Oscar for Best Documentary, Short Subjects, 1986.

[75] Evangelista, A. Synapse UCSF Student News-paper. Vol. 1, No. 20. 3 March 1977.

CHAPTER THIRTEEN — The First Campaign

[76] Luisa Buada, R.N, MPH is executive director of the Ravenswood Family Health Center, a free medical clinic offering health care for the medically underserved in East Palo Alto, California. The California Assembly named Luisa Buada "Woman of the Year" in 2018.

[77] 7 ALRB NO. 43 CASE No. 79-CL-6-SAL. UFW, AFL-CIO, Respondent. Salinas Marketing Co-op, et.al., Charging Parties. 5 September 1980.

[78] The National Migrant Referral Project 1975-1989 placed health centers for the Hispanic farmworker population. In 1989 the name was changed to the National Migrant Resource Program. The next iteration was as the National Center for Farmworker Health (NCFH) providing services to over 500 migrant health centers.

[79] Sakala, C. *Migrant and Seasonal Farmworkers in the United States: A Review of Health Hazards, Status, and Policy.* International Migrant Review. 1987 Fall; 21(3):659-87.

[80] Proposition 13 (People's Initiative to Limit Property Taxation) was an amendment to the Constitution of California enacted during 1978. Under the proposition the annual real estate tax on a parcel of property is limited to 1% of its assessed value.

[81]   Coalicion de Salud del Valle de Salinas provides health care services in Monterey County.

CHAPTER FOURTEEN-Fields of Poison

[82]   Ellenhorn, M.J., Barceloux, D.G. *Medical Toxicology-Diagnosis and Treatment of Human Poisoning.* Elsevier Science Publishing Co., New York. 1988. P. 1074. "Organophosphate poisoning is a problem in places where highly toxic organophosphorus pesticides are available. Medical management is difficult with case fatality generally more than 15%.

[83]   Dr. Molly Joel Coye, MD, MPH serves as Chief Innovation Officer UCLA Health System and heads the Institute for Innovation in Health and the Global Lab for Innovation at UCLA.

[84]   Coye, M. Journal of Public Health Policy. September 1985, Volume 6, Issue 3, pp. 349–370

[85]   Popovska-Gorevski, M, Dubocovich, M. L., Rajnarayan, R.V. *Carbamate Insecticides Target Human Melatonin Receptors.* Chem. Res. Toxicol, 2017, 30 (2), pp. 574–582.

[86]   Dr. Pablo Romero is a family medicine doctor in Salinas, California and is affiliated with Salinas Valley Memorial Hospital. He received his medical degree from University of California San Francisco School of Medicine.

[87]   Atropine does not provide complete protection from chemical nerve agents and insecticide poisoning. Drugs. com. *Atropine.*

[88]   Protopam Chloride is indicated as an antidote in the treatment of poisoning due to pesticides and chemicals (e.g., nerve agents) of the organophosphate class that have anticholinesterase activity. *National Institutes of Health.*

[89]   Cholinesterase is critical for the proper functioning of the nervous system. *Cholinesterase Inhibition.* Toxicology Information Brief. A Pesticide Information Project of Cooperative Extension Offices of Cornell University, Michigan State University, Oregon State University, and University of California at Davis. Major support and funding was provided by the USDA/Extension Service/National Agricultural Pesticide Impact Assessment Program. Oct. 1993

[90]   People, S. CFDA Health and Safety Memorandum. August 22, 1980.

CHAPTER FIFTEEN — A Passion for Justice

[91]   Mevinphos is a highly toxic organophosphate insecticide used on vegetables, primarily lettuce and cole crops. It was originally registered for use in 1957, but concerns about its safety arose quickly. After numerous discussions with the company that produced mevinphos, the Environmental Protection Agency cancelled its use on August 1, 1994.

[92]   Maddy, K.T., Smith, C., Updike, D. *Occupational Exposures to Mevinphos (Phosdrin) Reported by Physicians in California During 1980.* Worker Health and Safety Unit, Div. of Pest Management, Environmental Safety, and Worker Safety. California Dept. of Food and Agriculture, Sacramento, California. HS-873, July 22, 1981.

[93]   Brazil, E. *Demos bounce pesticide bills.* Salinas Californian via Gannett State Bureau. April 29, 1981.

[94]   Manning, H. *Poisoning case sentence reflects My Lai parallel.* Salinas Californian, May 11, 1981. p.1

[95]   Engstrom, P. *Workers examined for poisoning.* Salinas Californian. June 11, 1981.

[96]   Nutter, R., Agricultural Commissioner; Laurit-zen, E., Agricultural Commissioner Sealer of Weights & Measures Monterey County Posting Regulations, Effective May 5, 1983.

[97]   *San Jose Mercury. Pesticide warnings posted.* (AP) June 16, 1981, p. 4B.

[98]   Stahl, Z. *Field workers are still exposed to dangerous chemicals, 20 years after a landmark field-posting victory. Monterey County Weekly,* July 17, 2003.

CHAPTER SIXTEEN—Denial of Reality

[99]   House of Representatives, Subcommittee on Dept. Operations, Research, and Foreign Agriculture. *Federal*
246

Insecticide, Fungicide, and Rodenticide Act (Data and Trade Secret Issues). Tues., June 16, 1981. Pgs. 1-3.

[100]   Ibid. p. 11

[101]   Kibbe, P.R. Latin Americans in Texas. University of New Mexico Press, Albuquerque, New Mexico, 1948.

[102]   House of Representatives, Subcommittee on Dept. Operations, Research, and Foreign Agriculture. Federal Insecticide, Fungicide, and Rodenticide Act (Data and Trade Secret Issues). Tues., June 16, 1981. p. 137.

[103]   Ibid. p. 153

[104]   House of Representatives, Subcommittee on Dept. Operations, Research, and Foreign Agriculture. *Federal Insecticide, Fungicide, and Rodenticide Act (Safety, Health, Environmental Issues; Registration Process; Effects on International Pesticide Market)*. Thurs., July 16, 1981. Pgs. 201-202.

[105]   Pesticide drift is the airborne movement of pesticides from an area of application to any unintended site.

[106]   House of Representatives, Subcommittee on Dept. Operations, Research, and Foreign Agriculture. *Federal Insecticide, Fungicide, and Rodenticide Act (Safety, Health, Environmental Issues; Registration Process; Effects on International Pesticide Market)*. Thurs., July 16, 1981. 202-205

[107]   Ibid. p. 208.

108   Ibid. p. 212.

109   Ibid. p. 218.

110   Ibid. p. 274.

111   Ibid. p. 281.

112   Ibid. p. 292.

113   Ibid. Pgs. 342-343.

114   Ibid. Pgs. 360-361.

115   Ibid. p. 361.

116
        Ibid. p. 361.

117   Leon Panetta served in the House of Representatives, 1977-1993; Director of the Office of Budget and Management, 1993-1994; White House Chief of Staff, 1994-1997; Director of the CIA, 2009-2011; Secretary of Defense 2011-1013. Panetta co-founded the Panetta Institute for Public Policy at California State University, Monterey Bay, Monterey, California

118   *Advocates Seek Improved Protection*. Pesticides and You. Vol. 3, No. 1. June 1983.

[119]   Verticare Agricultural Helicopters was one of the largest crop-dusting companies in the Salinas Valley.

[120]   Engstrom, P. *ALRB workers exposed to pesticides.* Salinas Californian. July 17, 1982.

[121]   Engstrom, P. *Tests suggest workers exposed to pesticides.* Salinas Californian. July 21, 1982.

[122]   Letter from James T. Cheatham, President, Verticare Agricultural Helicopters to Marc del Piero, Clerk of the Board of Supervisors, Salinas, California. July 22, 1982.

[123]   Letter from E. G. Marshall President Soilserv, Inc. to William Peters, Clerk of the Board of Supervisors of Monterey County, Salinas, California. July 23, 1982.

[124]   Cheatham, J. *Public Forum: Aerial sprayer files a protest.* Salinas Californian. August 12, 1982.

[125]   Letter from Richard Andrews, Administrative Officer, Monterey County Administrative Management to Supervisor Marc Del Piero, Chairman, Board of Supervisors. Aug. 30, 1982.

[126]   Natividad Medical Center Memorandum to Monterey County Board of Supervisors from Ray K. Bolinger Natividad Hospital Administrator. Sept. 3, 1982.

[127]   California Dept. of food and Agriculture, Worker Health and Safety Unit, Sacramento, California. Regulations 2479; 2480. 1980.

[128]   Ira Monossan, M.D. a graduate of Stanford University School of Medicine left Cal/Osha in 1982. He practices Internal Medicine in the Los Angeles area.

[129]   Sharp, D.S. & Eskenazi, B., Harrison, R., Callas P. & Smith, A. H. *Delayed Health Hazards of Pesticide Exposure.* Annual Review Public Health 1986. 7:441-71.

[130]   Johnston, L., Asst. Dir. Pest Management, Environmental Protection and Worker Safety. *Notice of Pesticide Regulation Revision.* Dept. of Food and Agriculture. July 14, 1983.

[131]
Lightstone, R., Monning. W. M. *Comments on Proposed Amendments to Pesticide Worker Safety Regulations.* Aug. 12, 1983.

[132]   United States District Court Northern District of California, Sept. 15, 1983. Filed by Rucka, O'Boyle & Lombardo, Sept. 12, 1983.

[133]   Parsons, L. *Insecticide linked to birth defects.* Salinas Californian, March 16, 1984.

[134]   Parsons, L. *Farm workers win $278,000 settlement.* Salinas Californian, Sept. 11, 1984.

CHAPTER SEVENTEEN—Challenge and Vindication

135   *Cholinesterase Inhibition*. A Pesticide Information Project of Cooperative Extension Offices of Cornell University, Michigan State University, Oregon State University, and University of California at Davis. Sept. 1993.

136   Cheatham, J. *Public Forum: Pesticides get a bad rap.* Salinas Californian. Oct. 1, 1982.

137   Midtling, J.E. MD, MS; Barnett, P.G.; Coye, M. J. MD, MPH; Velasco, A. MD; Romero, P. MD; Clements, C.L. MD, MPH; O'Malley MD; Tobin, M. W. MD; Rose, T.G., MD; Monossan, I.H. MD. *Clinical Management of Field Worker Organophosphate Poisoning.* The Western Journal of Medicine. Apr. 1985, 142:514-518

138   California Department of Health Services. Remedial Action Order Docket No. HAS 86/87-003 RA. To: Verticare, a California Corporation; Verticare Agricultural Helicopters, Inc.; James T. and Julie A. Cheatham, Individuals. July 21, 1986.

Made in United States
Orlando, FL
20 November 2021

10561468R10157